Especially for

_____

From

_____

Date

_____

1

Published by Shiloh Run Press, an imprint of Barbour Publishing, Inc., P.O. Box
719, Uhrichsville, Ohio 44683, www.shilohrunpress.com

*Our mission is to publish and distribute inspirational products offering exceptional value
and biblical encouragement to the masses.*

Member of the
Evangelical Christian
Publishers Association

Printed in Canada.

When Jesus Speaks to a Woman's Heart

Donna K. Maltese

SHILOH RUN  PRESS
An Imprint of Barbour Publishing, Inc.

Introduction

♥♥♥♥♥♥♥♥♥♥

There is no doubt that in today's society, "women belonging to the Way" (Acts 9:2 AMP) can use all the support they can get to keep themselves whole, healthy, and holy on the narrow but joy-filled road. Hence, the book you now hold in your hands—*When Jesus Speaks to a Woman's Heart*—was written with you in mind.

The readings that follow will quench your spiritual thirst, uplift your sometimes bruised and battered heart, and give you more power and strength as you continue on your divine journey. Covering matters such as finances, worries, woes, dreams, priorities, and love, you will find encouragement, direction, and inspiration. Each devotion acts as a reminder that a woman is first and foremost on Jesus' mind and that there is no broken heart He cannot heal, no strength He cannot imbue, and no miracle He cannot perform.

Permit these pages to draw you closer to Jesus, and explore

- His presence in your life.
- His passion to save you.
- His plea for you to love and accept yourself as you are today.
- His purpose to empower you.
- His plan to help you become who you were meant to be.

♥ ♥ ♥ ♥ ♥ ♥ ♥ ♥ ♥

The Lord bless you and watch, guard, and keep you; the Lord make His face to shine upon and enlighten you and be gracious (kind, merciful, and giving favor) to you; the Lord lift up His [approving] countenance upon you and give you peace (tranquility of heart and life continually).

NUMBERS 6:24–26 AMP

Just Outside Your Door

❤ ❤ ❤ ❤ ❤ ❤ ❤ ❤ ❤ ❤

I am standing just outside your door, only a breath, a prayer, a sigh away. Are your ears open to the sound of My knock? Will you open the door of your heart, mind, and soul to the light of My presence?

Allow the noises and the distractions, within and without, to fade away. Come to Me for the peace that this world cannot give. Then you will hear My tap, tap, tapping. Then you will relax and listen to what I have to say. As you heed My voice, barriers between you and Me dissolve. The veil between Me and your heart, soul, and spirit dissipates. Here, within the flooding light of My presence, you find rest.

You have entered a place where the world can no longer touch you. You have come to Me, your

Shelter and your Refuge. You have sought My face and regained your soul. Tarry here for a little while longer. Breathe in My love and peace. Bask in My light. Then go in My strength, sated on Me, the Manna from heaven.

💜💜💜💜💜💜💜💜💜

Behold, I stand at the door and knock; if anyone hears and listens to and heeds My voice and opens the door, I will come in to him and will eat with him, and he [will eat] with Me.

REVELATION 3:20 AMP

This Is the Way

♥♥♥♥♥♥♥♥♥

There may be days when you are unsure of the next step on your journey. Let Me be your compass, giving you direction for every path you take.

Know that at any time you can come to Me for renewal, encouragement, strength, fortitude, and guidance. With a sure sense of Me by your side, you will learn how to act instead of react to each and every situation you encounter. With the kingdom of God within you, there is no need to worry about man's kingdom without.

Simply trust, assured that I will not lead you astray. As My Father did with Abraham, I will lead you to a place you may not yet be able to imagine. Yet it is the place I have designated and designed just for you. For there is no one else who can be the person you are, who can do what I have created you to do, who can go where I have called you to go.

From this point on, may your steps be sure. And if by chance any hesitation arises, look to Me. Listen to My soft voice say, "This is the way. Walk in it." Then go forward, knowing I am only a whisper away.

♥ ♥ ♥ ♥ ♥ ♥ ♥ ♥ ♥

Your ears will hear a word behind you, saying, This is the way; walk in it, when you turn to the right hand and when you turn to the left.

Isaiah 30:21 AMP

Above All Else

♥♥♥♥♥♥♥♥♥♥

You may be wondering why life can seem so hard sometimes, why you keep falling into the trap of fear, worry, and angst, why the world seems to be so upside down. It is because you are not seeking Me above everything else.

Each morning before your feet hit the floor, spend time with Me. Come into My presence and peace. Allow Me to fill your heart with My love, so much so that it will spill out onto those whose lives you touch.

Determine to view the world through My eyes, to see the light of God in each and every person. Rest in the assurance that all is well. I have laid out a perfect path for you. To find your way, you simply have to stop and ask directions. Be certain that no matter what happens, I am beside you. In My hand is everything you will ever need. Trust. Hope. Relax. Know that I am with you every step of the way.

Above all else in heaven and on earth, seek first My kingdom and My way of doing things, and everything else will fall into place.

♥♥♥♥♥♥♥♥♥

"Steep your life in God-reality, God-initiative, God-provisions. Don't worry about missing out. You'll find all your everyday human concerns will be met."

MATTHEW 6:33 MSG

Take Heart

♥ ♥ ♥ ♥ ♥ ♥ ♥ ♥ ♥ ♥

There is a time when a woman sees loved ones die, witnesses evil taking the upper hand, and experiences a despair that is almost too much to bear. But take heart. All this is simply an illusion—for I have conquered this world.

Believe that one day you will see your loved ones again. That one day you will see evil put in its place, and My goodness reign. Keep your faith that there is reason to hope in this land of the living.

Have a good cry if needed, and then dry your tears. When the grief begins to threaten once more and relief is desperately wanted, simply remind your heart, body, mind, and soul that all is well, that one day you will again see My goodness in this land, and that you need not concern

yourself with who, what, when, where, or why. But only come to Me and rest in My presence. Allow Me to fill you with courage and apply a healing balm to your heart. Simply wait, knowing these days of sorrow will pass and that the One who never changes will always be here for you, ready to wipe away your tears, replace your sorrowful sigh with laughter, and turn your grief into joy.

♥♥♥♥♥♥♥♥♥♥

I would have lost heart, unless I had believed that I would see the goodness of the LORD in the land of the living. Wait on the LORD; be of good courage, and He shall strengthen your heart; wait, I say, on the LORD!

PSALM 27:13–14 NKJV

Hidden Reserves

♥ ♥ ♥ ♥ ♥ ♥ ♥ ♥ ♥ ♥

There are some things you find difficult to do in your own strength. So turn to Me. I am here to help you live the life you have been called by our Father to live.

Dig deep into Me. I am your untapped power, your hidden reserves, your infinite supply. There is no need to look any further or to any other source. I hold more power than any food, drug, or superhero. And I hold it all for you.

So do not worry about anything. Just simply tap into Me. Fill yourself with supernatural strength and courage. Know that I am limited by neither time nor space. Thus I can go before you and be with you—all at the same time! And not just this once—but over and over again, and for all time!

I am your help in heaven and on earth. And I'm sticking close to you. Simply open up your heart and soul to My power and your eyes to My presence. Then walk forward—and keep walking. There is nothing to fear, nothing that can get you down when we are together.

♥ ♥ ♥ ♥ ♥ ♥ ♥ ♥ ♥

"Be strong and courageous. . . . The LORD himself goes before you and will be with you; he will never leave you nor forsake you. Do not be afraid; do not be discouraged."
DEUTERONOMY 31:7–8 NIV

In Step with God

My Word is not to be simply glossed over in the morning, a daily chore like making your bed. It is to be read slowly so that its strength and power will permeate your entire being—mind, body, spirit, and soul. This inspired wisdom is to be recalled day and night. Only in this way will it become a natural part of you. Only in this way can your thoughts even begin to parallel the thoughts of Father God.

As the Word becomes a part of you, you will thrive! You will no longer worry or fret but become peaceful of heart and mind. In such a relaxed state, you will make better decisions, knowing that whatever happens in a given situation, all will be well, for you are walking the right way—in step with Me. As you become imbued

with wisdom, success shall soon follow. You will be where you were meant to be and get to where you were destined to go.

♥ ♥ ♥ ♥ ♥ ♥ ♥ ♥ ♥

This Book of the Law shall not depart out of your mouth, but you shall meditate on it day and night, that you may observe and do according to all that is written in it. For then you shall make your way prosperous, and then you shall deal wisely and have good success.

JOSHUA 1:8 AMP

Spiritual Eyes

♥♥♥♥♥♥♥♥♥♥

In these moments with Me, gently close your eyes. Envision My presence beside you. Feel My breath upon your face. Bask in the warmth of My light. Your inner eyes are upon Me. Here there is no reason to fear or fret. In your powerlessness, you feel My strength. Breathe easy. Then commit these moments to memory.

In this power, in this memory, reopen your eyes. I am still with you—and always will be no matter what you face today. Don't worry about anything. Simply keep your spiritual eyes on Me. Know that I will never let anything harm you. Know that I will always be with you. Know that you don't have to always have the answer. Look to Me for all wisdom, strength, and power. For all I have is yours. And I have promised I will always

be here for you.

Thus, you may this day and all days walk forward in victory, no matter who or what is coming against you. Rest in My might, with your eyes upon Me. For in Me lie all answers.

♥ ♥ ♥ ♥ ♥ ♥ ♥ ♥ ♥ ♥

"For we have no power against this great multitude that is coming against us; nor do we know what to do, but our eyes are upon You."
2 CHRONICLES 20:12 NKJV

A Listening Ear

♥ ♥ ♥ ♥ ♥ ♥ ♥ ♥ ♥ ♥

I am ready to speak a good word to you. But sometimes you do not hear. Or you run the other way. Other times you will ask a friend for advice or seek an answer from books. Yet all the while I am vying for your attention.

I, wisdom personified, want to tell you what I am about to do in your life, in your world. Are you listening? Will you be My willing servant?

This relationship we have is not to be one- but two-sided. There is a time for you to speak and then a time for you to listen. And then not just listen, but obey.

I have a word for you, a woman after My own heart. You are also the apple of My eye. I see your face and smile, knowing how stupendous you are, if only you knew it, too.

When I come calling your name, open up your ears and heart. Respond with love and obedience. And then, "Behold!" Wondrous things will unfold.

♥♥♥♥♥♥♥♥♥

Now the LORD came and stood and called as at other times, "Samuel! Samuel!" And Samuel answered, "Speak, for Your servant hears." Then the LORD said to Samuel: "Behold. . ."
1 SAMUEL 3:10–11 NKJV

Dreams Arise

♥♥♥♥♥♥♥♥♥♥

At night, when there are more shadows than light, worries tend to creep into one's mind. Thought after thought seems to race through your head with no end in sight.

In the midst of your tossing, turn to Me. Remember Me. I am here, My arms stretched out wide, welcoming you to come to Me so that I may enfold you in a loving embrace.

Allow your worries—about the man you love, the children you care for, the friend you would lay down your life for—to fall away. Like an eagle that shelters her eaglets, I will cover you with My feathers. Here you are safe from all harm, all worries, all what-ifs.

I have promised you so much. And these promises are like a solid rock—unchangeable,

everlasting, certain, and sure. I will never leave
you. You are precious in My sight. Nothing is impossible for you. I bear your burdens—and do so
gladly.

Knowing all this, relax. Breathe deep. Trust in
Me. I will never let you fall. As the terrors of the
night fade away, beautiful dreams arise. Dream of
Me. Dream of love. Dream of peace.

♥ ♥ ♥ ♥ ♥ ♥ ♥ ♥ ♥

He will cover you with his feathers. He will
shelter you with his wings. His faithful promises
are your armor and protection. Do not be
afraid of the terrors of the night.

Psalm 91:4–5 nlt

Miracle Maker

♥♥♥♥♥♥♥♥♥

Woman, I am ready to do so many miracles in your life. Do you believe Me?

The greater your faith in Me, the more amazing things I can do in your life and in the lives of those around you. Do not limit Me. Train yourself to think outside the box. Humble yourself enough to believe in My grandeur. Push your doubts aside. Remember that I am the One who changed water into wine, healed lepers, calmed the sea and wind, and rose from the dead. There is nothing I *cannot* do—if your faith is big enough.

And once the miracle begins, it will continue for as long as you keep your eyes on Me. So do not look away, or you may sink down into the sea of doubt.

You are a woman of amazing strength. There

is no door closed to one who believes in the impossible. And that's My art—to make the impossible possible. Will you help Me? Will you not doubt? Will you believe anything can happen? If so, pray and petition. Watch and wait. Then praise and repeat.

♥ ♥ ♥ ♥ ♥ ♥ ♥ ♥ ♥

And he did not do many miracles there because of their lack of faith.

MATTHEW 13:58 NIV

Know Me

♥ ♥ ♥ ♥ ♥ ♥ ♥ ♥ ♥ ♥

I see you as no one else does. Your face, your hands, your size, your shape, your hair, your breath, your sigh—all these I know intimately. To Me, you are no stranger but an extension, an expression of Myself as you move in the light of love, forgiveness, and charity.

Yet at times, it seems I am yet a stranger to you. This will not do.

When you are worshipping or praying to Me, you cannot help but feel My love. Yet when you leave My presence, you sometimes leave Me and My love behind. My light and love are for you to not just experience in a moment of devotions but to carry back out into the world. How else will the world around you be changed?

So, friend and sister, seek Me out daily. Feel

the peace of My presence. Bask in the light of My love. Listen to the sound of My breath and My sigh. See Me as you have never seen Me before. Then take Me with you, out into the world. Become an extension of Me. Forgive the seemingly unforgivable. Love the unlovable. Help the helpless.

In doing so, you will begin to know Me as I know you—forever and ever, amen.

♥ ♥ ♥ ♥ ♥ ♥ ♥ ♥ ♥ ♥

"Before I shaped you in the womb, I knew all about you. Before you saw the light of day, I had holy plans for you."
JEREMIAH 1:5 MSG

Patience

♥ ♥ ♥ ♥ ♥ ♥ ♥ ♥ ♥

Thousands of earth years ago, an old woman named Sarah chuckled when Father God told her she and her elderly husband, Abraham, would birth a son. When He confronted her about her laughter, she denied mocking Him. But I knew. And so her patience was tested.

As time passed, Sarah became more and more impatient for a son. So she sought to take matters into her own hands and gave her servant Hagar over to Abraham, thinking this was how she, Sarah, would become a mother. Thus was born Ishmael through Hagar and Abraham. And trouble soon followed, first between the women and then between Sarah's promised son, Isaac, and his half brother Ishmael. Had she waited for the promise, much heartache would have been avoided.

Impatience often gives birth to trouble. And it comes about when you see the world through your eyes instead of Mine.

Believe Me when I tell you that I do all things at the perfect time. So rest easy. Do not try to force things to happen, but keep yourself in the flow of the river of life. I am the Living Water, the great Creator. I have you covered in each and every way. So do not go against My current but relax. Breathe. Lean back upon Me.

Your life and hopes are in My good hands. Trust and be satisfied in Me alone, and all your dreams will come true, all your hopes will be realized.

♥♥♥♥♥♥♥♥♥

Be still and rest in the Lord; wait for Him and patiently lean yourself upon Him.

Psalm 37:7 AMP

29

The Source of All

♥ ♥ ♥ ♥ ♥ ♥ ♥ ♥ ♥

I created woman to be a wonderful, flexible, nurturing vessel for humankind. It is through you that new lives may be created, fed in the womb, and nourished with love and affection that only a proper mother can give.

Yet you are also a fighter for the ones you love—from your children to your husband.

Yes, I have created you to become many things—a mother, sister, friend, wife, grandmother, coworker, teacher, and more. For you can be anything or anyone you put your mind to, like Deborah of old, who was not only a wife but a prophet, a judge, and a commander of Israel's army. The same love, foretelling, wisdom, and courage that were available to Deborah are available to you. Their source? Me—and Me alone.

So, My sister, come to Me now as the essential you—the daughter of the Lord Almighty. Strip yourself bare of all your varied roles, and focus only on what you as God's daughter need to face this day in strength and victory. This true you, this precious woman, will then receive all the love, foretelling, wisdom, and courage she needs to nurture, lead, and strengthen others in this day. For I, the source of all you need, will forever fill you up, day by precious day.

♥ ♥ ♥ ♥ ♥ ♥ ♥ ♥ ♥ ♥

Deborah, the wife of Lappidoth, was a prophet who was judging Israel at that time.

JUDGES 4:4 NLT

Working Out a Way

♥♥♥♥♥♥♥♥♥

I see all. I know exactly what your heart desires.
Yet I would have the words of your wants come
to Me by your own lips. Tell Me exactly what you
want. Show Me exactly what you desire. And I,
in return, will answer your prayer in accordance
with My wisdom.

You see, I see all things—not just your desires
but those of all My other brothers and sisters.
Like a child, you may desire something that may
not be good for you today, but perhaps it will be
tomorrow. So be patient. Continually pare down
your focus to what you truly desire with all your
mind, body, heart, and soul. And if it would be
good for you and the world, your desire shall be
granted.

Simply leave all in My hands and go forward,
knowing your Father will only give you what is

good and right for you in this time and space. And in the meantime, be content, knowing that I am working out a way for you to be all I created you to be—nothing more and nothing less than spectacular today and every day!

♥ ♥ ♥ ♥ ♥ ♥ ♥ ♥ ♥

Hannah prayed: I'm bursting with GOD-news! I'm walking on air. I'm laughing at my rivals. I'm dancing my salvation. Nothing and no one is holy like GOD, no rock mountain like our God. Don't dare talk pretentiously—not a word of boasting, ever! For GOD knows what's going on. He takes the measure of everything that happens.
1 SAMUEL 2:1–3 MSG

Pure Joy

♥ ♥ ♥ ♥ ♥ ♥ ♥ ♥ ♥

I am your Rock. Your Fortress. Your solid foundation! Do you see this?

When you come to Me, you seem to know Me. You recognize who I am and what I have done for you. But when you finish your prayers or devotions, you seem to leave Me where I am and try to live life in your own power! This shall not do!

Do you want joy? Do you want peace? Do you want strength? Do you want power? Then, My dear woman, remember that I am always looking out for you! I am always standing by your side! I see what you see—and so much more! So keep Me close. So close that you can hear Me breathe in rhythm with you. So close that you can hear Me whisper. So close that you can feel My power surging through you.

Knowing that I am with you, that I am eager to bless you, and that I am shielding you with all that I am will give you all the joy you could want—so much that it spills over you and onto others who may not yet know Me. With Me truly in your life and the light of your life, your pure joy cannot help but run over!

♥ ♥ ♥ ♥ ♥ ♥ ♥ ♥ ♥

Light is sown for the [uncompromisingly] righteous and strewn along their pathway, and joy for the upright in heart [the irrepressible joy which comes from consciousness of His favor and protection].

PSALM 97:11 AMP

Fallen Burdens

♥ ♥ ♥ ♥ ♥ ♥ ♥ ♥ ♥

So many people are weighed down by the past. They constantly mull over in their minds, *If only I had done this.* Or *If only I could take that back.* Such thoughts get them nowhere.

Each day is a new day, a new beginning. Forget what happened (or didn't happen) yesterday. Come to Me in this moment. Focus only on Me. There is no use in rehashing the could'ves, would'ves, and should'ves. It's time to reach for the things ahead of you.

That is the ultimate freedom, the path to peace, the road to well-being. Shed that burden that you have been carrying. Let it fall from your shoulders and onto Mine. That is what I came here for. That is the freedom My path allows you. That's what enables you to be an effective worker

for Me. For only when the burden has fallen will you be open to receive more and more blessings.

So, woman, forgive all those who have wronged you—including yourself. Let go of all the memories that give you pain. Forget about the what-ifs. Then breathe deeply the air of freedom, the scent of your Christ, who came to free you from every kind of bondage, including burdens that are in reality merely dust.

♥ ♥ ♥ ♥ ♥ ♥ ♥ ♥ ♥ ♥

One thing I do, forgetting those things which are behind and reaching forward to those things which are ahead.
PHILIPPIANS 3:13 NKJV

Streaming Thoughts

♥ ♥ ♥ ♥ ♥ ♥ ♥ ♥ ♥

You must train yourself, My child, to be a witness to the thoughts that are streaming through your head. The negative thoughts are only shadows of reality, mucking up your mind. Do not let them have sway or power over you. Instead, let them flow through unheeded. Pay no attention to the fear, panic, hatred, lust, grief, and aggression they bring with them. Just allow them to pass away. If more strength is needed, simply call on Me. When you say My name, "Jesus," My light makes all shadows disperse. All evil fades. For it has no strength, no power against Me.

Just keep your mind on Me. Hand over your entire self—mind, body, spirit, soul. I will keep you safe from all harm. I will give you all the joy and strength you need. You need not look anywhere else.

Feed on Me, your Bread of life. Drink of Me, your Living Water. Come to Me, your Burden Bearer, eternal Friend, Light of the world. Rest assured that I will never leave you, fail you, forsake you. And that's the truth. That's My promise and your confidence.

♥ ♥ ♥ ♥ ♥ ♥ ♥ ♥ ♥

You will guard him and keep him in perfect and constant peace whose mind [both its inclination and its character] is stayed on You, because he commits himself to You, leans on You, and hopes confidently in You.

ISAIAH 26:3 AMP

Always Present

♥♥♥♥♥♥♥♥♥

You have had your sorrows and temptations in this life, as well as heartbreak, rejection, and derision. And through it all, whether you knew it or not, whether you recognized Me or not, I was walking with you.

In the midst of your fire, I felt the flame. In the midst of your flood, I felt the undercurrent. In the midst of your earthquake, I felt the earth tremble.

No matter where you are, no matter what happens, I am walking this road with you. So stop. Take a rest. Call My name—and then you will see Me. Then you will know that I've been right next to you all along.

Thus there is no reason to dread the fires, floods, or earthquakes in your life. There is no

reason to let them shake you up. You can be confident in Me, My presence, My strength. I am holding on to you tightly and will never ever let you go. Simply put your hand in Mine, and walk on. The Son of God is walking with you.

♥ ♥ ♥ ♥ ♥ ♥ ♥ ♥ ♥

"Look!" he answered, "I see four men loose, walking in the midst of the fire; and they are not hurt, and the form of the fourth is like the Son of God."

DANIEL 3:25 NKJV

Future Plans

♥♥♥♥♥♥♥♥♥♥

You need not worry about anything. Truly, I have it all planned out for you, every aspect of your life. All you need to do is continually tap into Me. Ask Me about each and every move you make. If you feel uncomfortable about something, stop. Have you spoken to Me about it, asked Me if it was a part of the plan for your life?

Whenever you need to make a decision, come to Me first. I will give you the wisdom you need to move forward. Everything I have in mind is for your good. When you make Me—and only Me—your Source, your Hope, your Rock, your Refuge, your Shield, your Strength, your Light, you are on the path to the kingdom of God. And as you walk that road, you are walking with Me. Your future is safe, assured, and perfect. For your future is Me.

So lift yourself above the cares of this world. Gently lay your head upon My shoulder. Rest in My embrace. Feed yourself upon My strength. Know that I will never leave you or forsake you. You need never walk alone.

♥ ♥ ♥ ♥ ♥ ♥ ♥ ♥ ♥ ♥

"I know what I'm doing. I have it all planned out—plans to take care of you, not abandon you, plans to give you the future you hope for."
JEREMIAH 29:11 MSG

Love—Pure and Unfettered

♥♥♥♥♥♥♥♥♥

There are some things (and some people) you may never be able to change. But that is not your affair. Your business is loving all—no matter who they are or what they do. For didn't I love you when you were still confused and ignorant of My presence and My ways?

The best way to show others the Way is to shower them with the love you get from Me. That's why I've asked you to feed the hungry, clothe the naked, visit the prisoner. While you are at it, do something nice for the intrusive mother-in-law, the demanding boss, the unfriendly neighbor, the gum-cracking checkout girl, the desperate-looking homeless man. Find a way to reach the heart of others by tapping into My reserves. Each kindness you bestow upon

another restores My reserves and comes back at you a hundredfold.

So don't let others irritate. Instead allow them to help you navigate your way through this world. Let them be markers on your road to paradise. Let them see our love for what it is—pure and unfettered.

Who can you bless this way? Who can you love today?

♥♥♥♥♥♥♥♥♥♥

*But God showed his great love
for us by sending Christ to die for
us while we were still sinners.*

ROMANS 5:8 NLT

45

Lost, Now Found

♥♥♥♥♥♥♥♥♥♥

There is no need for you to hide your face from Me, for I know what you've been doing. I know what you've been going through, how you gave in to temptation, erred in your speech, or made a gross mistake in some other way. And in spite of all the harm you think you've done or the heartache you may have caused yourself or others, know this: I am filled with compassion for you.

For a little while you were lost, but now you are found. You are back in My presence. There may, of course, be some repercussions from your actions, for as you know, you reap what you sow. But also know this—I am celebrating your return, no matter how short or long your absence was! This is because I adore you. Because I do have such great plans for you. Because there is nothing more

wonderful than a sheep coming back to the fold.

So do not think I am angry. Do not think I am disgusted with you. Believe Me when I tell you I am overjoyed at your return. And I am thrilled that you are focusing on Me once again.

You have learned a hard lesson. But you have returned to the kingdom of God. I'm so happy you're home. And that is something to celebrate!

♥♥♥♥♥♥♥♥♥

*"So he returned home to his father.
And while he was still a long way off,
his father saw him coming. Filled with
love and compassion, he ran to his son,
embraced him, and kissed him."*

Luke 15:20 nlt

47

The Light

♥♥♥♥♥♥♥♥♥

Rest your body. Sit back in your chair. Put your feet flat on the floor. Relax. Allow My light and life to fill you from the top of your head to the bottom of your feet.

Breathe easy. One breath, then two, then three. Let all the troubles of the world fade away. Whatever has happened, has happened. Whatever will be, will be. Let it go. Drift away from the earthly world. Rise up to the kingdom of God.

Come to Me now. In My presence there is peace. Here you are surrounded by a love that can never die. Here there is no sorrow or pain. There is only a light that glows like no other. It is the light of a life with Me.

You, too, can have this light. It's a light that you can shine into the earthly world. It's a light that will point others to Me. Let this light shine.

Let it fill you to overflowing. Let it lead you to all good things.

Rest here for a moment or two longer. Then, as you slowly return to the earthly world, remember the light that you have within. Keep the flame alive by spreading My love. Keep the darkness at bay. Be still. Know that I am God—and that you are the light of this world.

♥ ♥ ♥ ♥ ♥ ♥ ♥ ♥ ♥

Let be and be still, and know (recognize and understand) that I am God.

PSALM 46:10 AMP

The Remedy

♥♥♥♥♥♥♥♥♥♥

Gently, gently lift your head. There is no sorrow so deep that I cannot heal it. No pain so great I cannot remedy it. Come to Me. Put your entire self—not just your mind or just your body, but your mind, body, soul, and spirit—in My hands. Release from yourself any distrust, doubt, and despair as air from a balloon, until there is no debility remaining that would hinder My work, until there is nothing left but a foundation of freedom, a time of rest, and a spark of hope. Then allow Me to build you back up as you abide in Me and My Spirit abides in you. I am your healer. I am your remedy. I am the answer to all your questions. Remain in this secret place with Me. Know that I am the greatest and mightiest force in heaven and on earth. With Me you are vulnerable yet safe; you are home yet a foreigner in a strange

place; you are alone yet surrounded by Me and a heavenly host.

♥ ♥ ♥ ♥ ♥ ♥ ♥ ♥ ♥

But you have come to Mount Zion,
to the city of the living God, the heavenly
Jerusalem. You have come to thousands upon
thousands of angels in joyful assembly....
You have come to God, the Judge of all...
to Jesus the mediator of a new covenant.
HEBREWS 12:22–24 NIV

The Journey Ahead

In My strength, you have been victorious. And now you have come off the mountaintop and into this wilderness, exhausted, depressed, and alone. Upon your lips are the words of Elijah: "I've had enough, LORD." You may rest here until you regain your strength and joy.

Upon a touch from My angel, I will awaken you and give you Myself—the Water and Bread of life—for your nourishment. Once you are sated, this spiritual food will give you untold strength so you can continue the work you were designed to do. I will lead you out of this wilderness. I will clear the way ahead. I will give you the next path you are to take. But for now, worry not. Simply know that My angel is watching over you on the first and last steps of each and every path you take, from mountaintop to valley to wilderness to mountaintop again. And know that all the spiritual nourishment you truly need for the journey ahead is found in Me.

♥♥♥♥♥♥♥♥♥♥

Then the angel of the LORD came again and touched him and said, "Get up and eat some more, or the journey ahead will be too much for you." So he got up and ate and drank, and the food gave him enough strength to travel forty days and forty nights.

1 KINGS 19:7–8 NLT

From Dawn to Dusk

♥ ♥ ♥ ♥ ♥ ♥ ♥ ♥ ♥ ♥

Do not be a stranger. As the day breaks, come into My presence. Then linger with Me for a moment. Allow Me to be your morning provision. I am—and have—all you need to face each and every day. If given the opportunity, I will richly nourish your spirit, strengthen your body, spark your mind, and gladden your soul. All this I, the risen Son, will give you before you step one foot on the ground. It is a feast treasured by many saved souls.

So do not bypass these precious moments. Come. Linger. Open yourself to My supply that will fortify you throughout your day.

And then when day is done, the sun has set, come to Me once again. Do not be afraid of the darkness. There is no shadow that can separate us. So lay yourself down. Breathe easy upon your bed. Envision Me beside you once more. Thank Me for the countless blessings you received from My hand. Say a prayer for your family and friends. Then enter the sleep of the innocent. And may your gentle smile be the precursor to the joy of the dreams you are about to witness.

♥♥♥♥♥♥♥♥♥

What a beautiful thing, GOD, to give thanks,
to sing an anthem to you, the High God!
To announce your love each daybreak, sing your
faithful presence all through the night.

PSALM 92:1–2 MSG

Dreams

♥♥♥♥♥♥♥♥♥♥

Why do you continue to try to do everything in your own power? Why do you not ask Me for advice, direction, help? You act as if I am to have no part in helping your dreams to come true. Or that you need to carry all the burden of attaining your dream on your own shoulders, as if your strength is the end-all and be-all. Instead of carrying this entire load by yourself, come to Me. Tell Me what your dreams and aspirations are—and why. Lay them in My tender hands. Then rest well in the knowledge that I will enlighten you. That I will give you the wisdom to make the right decisions, to take the right path. I will help you to determine what is best for your life—as well as the people in it. When you bare your heart before Me, when you tell Me everything that is on your

mind, when you open up to Me as to no other, I cannot help but be moved. So don't hold back. Tell Me all, and I will help you make all your dreams a reality!

💜 💜 💜 💜 💜 💜 💜 💜 💜

Commit your way to the Lord [roll and repose each care of your load on Him]; trust (lean on, rely on, and be confident) also in Him and He will bring it to pass.

PSALM 37:5 AMP

Mighty Power

♥♥♥♥♥♥♥♥♥♥

Like Elijah in the cave, you have hidden yourself away, are sleeping in the darkness, and are licking your wounds. What are you doing here? From what are you fleeing? Have people abused you? Has your faith deserted you? Has the dark one convinced you that he is stronger than Father, Son, and Holy Spirit? Have you given up on the world? Are you feeling overwrought, overshadowed, overcome?

Wake up, woman! Have you forgotten that you are the daughter of God the King? That you wear His armor? That you have access to mountain-moving faith? Get back on solid spiritual ground through the Word. Allow the clamor of the world to fall away as you seek Me in prayer. Then, restored and renewed, come out of the shadows

and into the pillar of My light. Open your eyes and seek My face. Open your ears and hear My gentle whisper. You have My resurrection power. Thus nothing is impossible for you. You are a child of the light—not a cave dweller!

♥♥♥♥♥♥♥♥♥

I also pray that you will understand the incredible greatness of God's power for us who believe him. This is the same mighty power that raised Christ from the dead and seated him in the place of honor at God's right hand in the heavenly realms.

Ephesians 1:19–20 NLT

When Tempers Flare

♥♥♥♥♥♥♥♥♥♥

I, your Lord and Master, know the thoughts you think. I know what runs through your head after you've had a heated discussion. But I also know your heart. You are a good woman, mother, worker, sister, daughter, wife, and friend. You have no desire to intentionally hurt anyone or anything. Yet sometimes words seem to fly out of your mouth. And before you know it, they've sparked a firestorm. Sometimes it's not really even the words themselves but the tone of voice, the volume level, or the unable-to-be-hidden intent that comes glaring through. And now you, although you may still be a little angry or upset, are sorry for what you said, for losing your temper. Don't be afraid to confess your feelings to Me or to apologize to the one you think you may have hurt. Although it may be humbling to ask forgiveness, or to even admit that you have done something wrong, you will be filled with so much more joy afterward.

So tell Me all your troubles. Know that I understand. And then go with My strength and blessing to the one your words have hurt. Go in My name, and may My forgiveness and joy go with you, regardless of how your apology is received. For loving others—by word and deed—is always the right thing to do.

♥♥♥♥♥♥♥♥♥

"In your anger do not sin": Do not let the sun go down while you are still angry, and do not give the devil a foothold.
EPHESIANS 4:26–27 NIV

A New Road

♥♥♥♥♥♥♥♥♥♥

Are you ready for a new challenge? Are you following My lead, My promptings, My direction? Do you see the new thing I am leading you to? Too often My sisters miss the open door I have before them. Sometimes it is because they are focused more on the treasures of the earth than the treasures of heaven. Or they are too self-absorbed in their own plans, never looking up to see what I'm doing. But here I am, opening a door for you. There is a new path, a new opportunity for you. Don't miss it!

Forget about the things that happened in the past. This is a new day! It is a new way! Stop for a moment. Look up. Ask Me what I would have you do, where I would have you go. Heed My voice. Listen to My direction. Take off your blinders. Open up your mind and your eyes. Then look around you. There is a new road. Take the first step into the adventure awaiting you. Know that I am with you and will continue to guide you in this new endeavor. Use Me as your GPS—and be amazed at what unfolds!

♥♥♥♥♥♥♥♥♥

"Forget about what's happened; don't keep going over old history. Be alert, be present. I'm about to do something brand-new. It's bursting out! Don't you see it? There it is! I'm making a road through the desert, rivers in the badlands."

ISAIAH 43:18-19 MSG

Listen

♥♥♥♥♥♥♥♥♥

You were never meant to walk this road alone. That is one reason I came to earth, to show you the way and to leave you with a companion, a Comforter, the Holy Spirit. But you also have fellow human travelers, who appear in so many different roles—as mentor, teacher, adviser, friend, husband, brother, sister, mother, father. Each one can teach you in his or her own special way. They are here for you on your journey—and you are here for them on theirs.

So be as gentle with them as you would want them to be with you. Help lift their load—as they help you carry yours. Reach out to them as I reach out to you. Comfort, protect, forgive, inspire, and encourage them—but most of all, pay attention to what they have to say.

One of the greatest ways to show your love is to truly listen to others in your life without judgment or criticism. Simply focus on the part of Me you see in them, and listen as you would have Me listen to you—not letting one precious word drop to the floor unheard.

♥ ♥ ♥ ♥ ♥ ♥ ♥ ♥ ♥

Live creatively, friends. If someone falls into sin, forgivingly restore him, saving your critical comments for yourself. You might be needing forgiveness before the day's out. Stoop down and reach out to those who are oppressed. Share their burdens, and so complete Christ's law.

GALATIANS 6:1–2 MSG

Dieter's Delight

♥♥♥♥♥♥♥♥♥♥

Don't just rush through your daily devotions. Dig deep down. Be still and silent, and allow My Word to simmer. Make it a part of your daily diet, chewing slowly so you thoroughly digest each and every letter, word, sentence, paragraph, and page. For when you do, those words become a part of your very being, able to be recalled at a moment's notice, saving you from darkness and disaster, lifting you high above earthly troubles, and giving you much-needed strength.

The words of scripture—new and old—renew, refresh, and re-create you down to the core. They satisfy you like nothing else on this earth. They are to be your food and drink. Your very nourishment. Your manna from heaven. The more those words become a part of your life, the more you

know and understand your Lord and Master, and the more I truly become a part of your world. The more time you spend in the Word, the more you will gain delight and joy. Happy and blessed is the woman whose regular diet is soul food.

♥ ♥ ♥ ♥ ♥ ♥ ♥ ♥ ♥ ♥

"When I discovered your words, I devoured them. They are my joy and my heart's delight."

JEREMIAH 15:16 NLT

First Come, Always Served

♥♥♥♥♥♥♥♥♥

Where are you looking for help? To things, other people, money, or institutions? Don't you know that they are all fallible? That none of them are unchangeable, eternal, and filled with the awesome power of God? Do you not know the only thing that can truly save you is Me?

Look to Me—and Me alone—for each and every need! Even though getting you out of the pit *seems* impossible, nothing is too difficult for Me! Can you not wait for Me to rescue you in My own timing? Don't look for other "things" to save you right here and now. Be patient! I have bigger plans in mind for you.

Do you need something to believe in? Don't fall for that false American idol. Look to Me. Do you need or want a man in your life? Don't give yourself to every Tom, Dick, and Harry, but give yourself more fully to Me. Do you need financial help?

Come to Me. Have faith that I will provide. Do you need employment? Checking the want ads is fine, but come to Me first. I will open doors you had no clue even existed.

Look to Me before all things, believe in My power—and watch great plans unfold! When you consistently come first to Me, you will always be served!

♥♥♥♥♥♥♥♥♥

What sorrow awaits those who look to Egypt for help, trusting their horses, chariots, and charioteers and depending on the strength of human armies instead of looking to the LORD, the Holy One of Israel.

ISAIAH 31:1 NLT

Word Power

♥ ♥ ♥ ♥ ♥ ♥ ♥ ♥ ♥

So you were going along fine, and then you read something in My Word that has stopped you in your tracks. My daughter, this is a good thing! This Word that you read each and every day is alive! It is speaking directly to your soul! It reaches where nothing else can! It is pointing out something in your life that you need to address. Perhaps there is a friend or neighbor you need to apologize to, a wrong you have been avoiding but need to right. Perhaps there is a child or a younger woman looking for guidance, hope, and direction. Perhaps you have been storing more treasures on earth than in heaven and priorities need to be shifted. Perhaps it is something that goes much deeper, something you cannot quite discern. In each of these cases, there is a reason to praise! I am speaking directly to your life!

I and the Word—one and the same—are indeed alive, leading you, guiding you, helping you. Spend some more time in meditation with Me today. Apply to My wisdom. Ask, seek, knock—then you will know and all things will be set right.

❤❤❤❤❤❤❤❤❤

For the Word that God speaks is alive and full of power [making it active, operative, energizing, and effective]; it is sharper than any two-edged sword, penetrating to the dividing line of the breath of life (soul) and [the immortal] spirit, and of joints and marrow [of the deepest parts of our nature], exposing and sifting and analyzing and judging the very thoughts and purposes of the heart.

HEBREWS 4:12 AMP

Overflowing Blessings

♥♥♥♥♥♥♥♥♥

You are like every good woman, oftentimes driven to nurture and care for others before nurturing or caring for yourself. Yet living thus may weaken you, not only physically, mentally, and emotionally, but spiritually as well. Take this moment to reevaluate your life. Come before Me and be totally honest. Where are you giving most of yourself—to your job, your family, your husband, your friends, your education, your church? If so, stop. Reconsider.

Give your all first to Me, your Lord and Savior. Bring all your tithes—your talents, hopes, dreams, love, passion, gifts, mind, soul, spirit—to Me. Put them in My possession. Trust Me with all that you are, have, and ever hope to be. Then see what happens!

Watch how the windows of heaven will open and pour blessing upon blessing into your life. Let

go of all you are holding on to—doubts, worries, fears, possessions, money, jealousies, nightmares, anger, confusion, fear, memories, grief, stress, feelings of unworthiness—so that you can open up your hands to capture all the gifts I am bursting to give you. Give to Me until I overflow onto you.

❤ ❤ ❤ ❤ ❤ ❤ ❤ ❤ ❤

Bring all the tithes (the whole tenth of your income) into the storehouse, that there may be food in My house, and prove Me now by it, says the Lord of hosts, if I will not open the windows of heaven for you and pour you out a blessing, that there shall not be room enough to receive it.

MALACHI 3:10 AMP

73

Time of Testing

♥♥♥♥♥♥♥♥♥

When you go through a time of testing, do not despair. There will be better days ahead. For now, simply know that I am with you every step of the way. If you cannot get over, under, or around an obstacle, I will help you get through it. All I require of you is faith.

Believe that I am holding your hand, that I have a firm grip on you and will never let you go. When darkness comes and panic begins to set in, feel My tug and allow your heart to calm. Know that everything will turn out all right, that through this testing, you are growing and learning. Once you are out on the other side, you will know the landscape of this particular trial so well that you will be able to help others through it. So don't worry about the what-ifs. Don't speculate on what might've been. Simply take deep breaths. Remember the times I have gotten you through in the past. Keep in mind all the things I did to save you—and know that I am not about to let go of you now. Be firm in these thoughts. And you will feel My peace break through, from My Spirit to yours.

♥♥♥♥♥♥♥♥♥

"For I am the LORD your God who takes hold of your right hand and says to you, Do not fear; I will help you. Do not be afraid."

ISAIAH 41:13–14 NIV

A Stretch of Faith

❤ ❤ ❤ ❤ ❤ ❤ ❤ ❤ ❤

I, Jesus Christ, can do anything, for I am God's one and only Son. So why is it that, at times, you limit Me? If only you had the faith of the commander I met thousands of years ago. He desired healing for his servant boy. That in itself is commendable, that this centurion would come and chase Me down for a blessing for a young servant. But what was even more commendable was that he said all I had to do was say the word—and he knew the boy would be cured!

Do you have that faith? Do you trust that all I have to do is say the word and what you believe will be done—in the twinkling of an eye? When I was walking among you, God in the form of flesh, I healed many, many people of illness. I walked on water. I calmed the sea and the wind.

I turned water into wine. I made the blind to see, the lame to walk. I withered a fig tree with mere words. When My disciples saw it, they marveled. And My words to them are the same words I am now saying to you: "Have a constant faith in God. And whatever you believe will take place will be done." The same goes for you, woman. Constantly be stretching your faith and watch amazing things unfold.

❤ ❤ ❤ ❤ ❤ ❤ ❤ ❤ ❤

Then Jesus said to the centurion, "Go!
Let it be done just as you believed it would."
And his servant was healed at that moment.

MATTHEW 8:13 NIV

Divine Inspiration

♥ ♥ ♥ ♥ ♥ ♥ ♥ ♥ ♥ ♥

There are so many things you probably don't understand about God the Father, the Holy Spirit, and Me. And yet you really don't need to understand all to believe. All you really need to know is that I make the invisible visible. That the eagle climbs at My command. The seasons change at My calling. As winter approaches, I send some birds south. Through My power, the earth, moon, sun, and stars maintain their orbits. I know and understand this world, from the depths of the earth to the farthest reaches in the sky. I know each forest, pasture, mountain, valley, city, town, oasis, and desert. I know down to the last atom every living thing I have created—including you. There is nothing you can hide from Me. There is no question that I cannot answer.

All I ask of you is to have faith in Me. To

understand that when I speak, things happen. To believe that everything I create and have created has its purpose. Yours is to worship Me. To love Me with all your heart, soul, strength, and mind. To love others as you love yourself. Begin to live your purpose. Let nothing stand in your way. Simply look to Me. Seek My face. Love—and be loved. Follow in My footsteps. Become My divine inspiration.

❤ ❤ ❤ ❤ ❤ ❤ ❤ ❤ ❤

By faith we understand that the worlds [during the successive ages] were framed (fashioned, put in order, and equipped for their intended purpose) by the word of God, so that what we see was not made out of things which are visible.

HEBREWS 11:3 AMP

A Praiseworthy Mind-Set

♥♥♥♥♥♥♥♥♥

Feeling stuck? If so, your head is too much in this world and not enough in Mine. Lift yourself out of the darkness and into the light of My Word. Consider those women who have gone before, the heroes of old—Miriam, Deborah, Rahab, Esther, Abigail, Naomi, and Ruth. And the heroes of new—Elizabeth, Mary, Mary Magdalene, Joanna, Lydia, and Lois. Remember their faith, commitment, strength, perseverance, courage, and confidence.

Look away from the flood. Seek the rainbow. Keep your mind off the sinners, and focus on the saints. Do not allow yourself to be swallowed by the shadows of this earth. But strain your ears to hear a good word—and may your mouth be eager to give a good word back. Do not become bowed down by the burdens of the world. Instead, allow them to slip off your back as you rise up to the ways of love and the Lord. Stay in tune with the heavenly harmonies of Father God, and you will be in sync with His angels.

♥♥♥♥♥♥♥♥♥

Friends, I'd say you'll do best by filling your minds and meditating on things true, noble, reputable, authentic, compelling, gracious—the best, not the worst; the beautiful, not the ugly; things to praise, not things to curse. Put into practice what you learned from me, what you heard and saw and realized. Do that, and God, who makes everything work together, will work you into his most excellent harmonies.

PHILIPPIANS 4:8–9 MSG

Refuge

♥♥♥♥♥♥♥♥♥

When you are sore and weary, run to Me. When you are tired of your frantic pace, run to Me. When you are frightened, confused, and over-whelmed by the darkness of this world, run to Me. When you can no longer read My Word through your tears, run to Me. When you feel that all is lost and you can no longer go on, run to Me—for I am.

I am all the nourishment you need, for I am your Living Water and miraculous Manna. I am all the protection you need, for I am your breast-plate. I am all the comfort you could want, for no shoulder is bigger than Mine. I, your Strong Tower, am your Shelter in the mightiest of storms. Here in My presence, no evil can touch you. Nothing can penetrate My shield of love for the people who are called by My name.

So in your time of trial, turn to no one but Me. And you will rest secure in My everlasting arm that is never too short to pull you out of danger and into My protective hold. Come. Abide in Me as I abide in My Father. Here you may rest. Here you will come to no harm. Here you shall remain until you have been restored and are ready to go on.

♥ ♥ ♥ ♥ ♥ ♥ ♥ ♥ ♥

The name of the Lord is a strong tower;
the [consistently] righteous man [upright and
in right standing with God] runs into it
and is safe, high [above evil] and strong.

PROVERBS 18:10 AMP

Banked Promises

♥♥♥♥♥♥♥♥♥♥

Has My Word fallen on deaf ears, distracted minds, drained hearts, defiant souls, and diverted spirits? If so, how will you be able to defend yourself from malicious slander, worldly "wisdom," misdirected love, and societal evil? I implore you, daughter of God, to take the Word deep into your very being. Open your ears to hear each nuance, to understand each intention of the Holy Spirit who strives to communicate, to make everything clear to you. Focus your mind by memorizing those verses that have truly reached your soul. Allow them to become a part of your being, to penetrate to the heart of your matter, and so fill it with life-giving power and love. Open up your soul to the absolute truth and wisdom of Me so that I truly become your one and only Lord and Savior.

This is how you will find yourself unable to be

touched or tempted by evil, how you will become wise in all ways of living and be seen as one of God's own. And in these ways attract others to the God who fills your entire being, giving your open ears a good word, your focused mind food for thought, your empty heart overflowing love, your soul the blessings that come with obedience, and your spirit the joy of abiding and joining with Me.

♥ ♥ ♥ ♥ ♥ ♥ ♥ ♥ ♥ ♥

*I've banked your promises in the vault of my
heart so I won't sin myself bankrupt. Be blessed,
GOD; train me in your ways of wise living.
I'll transfer to my lips all the counsel
that comes from your mouth.*
PSALM 119:11–13 MSG

Food for Thought

♥♥♥♥♥♥♥♥♥♥

Thoughts are very powerful things, for from them material things are birthed. So, dear sister, about what are you thinking?

Consider Job. He fed his thoughts on his fears—and what he feared ended up coming upon him. Some people feed on worries—and those worries come upon them. Some feed on sickness—and catch every illness that can be caught. When you get it into your mind that you're going to have a bad day, chances are you are calling a bad day into being. But this should not be so! You have at your fingertips an amazing resource to keep your troubles at bay. It is My Word.

Fill your mind with reassurances of My love. See yourself protected in My arms. Sing My psalms, and rise up in faith. Follow the proverbs, and walk forward in wisdom. Make the words of My Sermon on the Mount part of your life and that life will be blessed. Consistently read, believe, think about, and walk in My words, and birth a world of beauty, light, and abundance.

♥ ♥ ♥ ♥ ♥ ♥ ♥ ♥ ♥

For the thing which I greatly fear comes upon me, and that of which I am afraid befalls me. I was not or am not at ease, nor had I or have I rest, nor was I or am I quiet, yet trouble came and still comes [upon me].

JOB 3:25–26 AMP

Spiritual Seeds

♥♥♥♥♥♥♥♥♥♥

Every farmer knows that whatever he plants, that is what he will reap. If he plants seeds of wheat, he will harvest wheat. If he plants corn, he will harvest corn. It also follows that the more seed a farmer sows, the bigger his crop. These are both physical laws. But they are also a reflection of spiritual laws. If you sow seeds of discord, that is what you will reap. It is the same with seeds of discontent, dishonor, and disappointment. Once a seed sown, it cannot help but be reaped. And the more of something you sow, the more of that you will harvest.

So I ask you, dear sister, what are you planting in your life? What crops are coming up for you—and in what amount? Know that you cannot fool God. He sees, feels, and hears what you are planting— and He is giving you the same in return. So dig deep into the Word. Meditate on its meaning. Then, with the help of the Holy Spirit, plant spiritual seeds of love, joy, peace, and patience in your life. Add kindness, goodness, and faithfulness. Make room for gentleness and self-control. And come harvesttime, you will find spiritual fruit that you—and those around you—can grow on!

♥♥♥♥♥♥♥♥♥

Do not be deceived: God cannot be mocked. A man reaps what he sows. Whoever sows to please their flesh, from the flesh will reap destruction; whoever sows to please the Spirit, from the Spirit will reap eternal life.

GALATIANS 6:7–8 NIV

The Wisdom of God

♥♥♥♥♥♥♥♥♥

Do not lose hope and faith if you are mocked or called foolish because of your belief in Me and My Word. Even My disciples had trouble totally understanding what I was doing while on earth. When told I had risen again, the Eleven thought the words of the women were nonsense. But that did not take away the power and effect of the truth of the matter. And I am the Way, the Truth, and the Life. All of My Word reveals the power of God. It brings to light His wisdom—even though it seems like foolishness to the world of men.

Know that even if your mind cannot understand the who, what, when, where, why, and how of the Gospel and all that preceded it, it matters not. For God, through Me and My Word, has saved, is saving, and will save all who believe

in Me. He has made you His daughter through faith in Me. What else is there to know? Simply believe in the Word. Believe in its power. And as you continue to walk with God, Me, and the Holy Spirit, your life will, in the eyes of this foolish world, become an extraordinary example of the supernatural power of God.

♥♥♥♥♥♥♥♥♥

To those whom God has called, both Jews and Greeks, Christ the power of God and the wisdom of God. For the foolishness of God is wiser than human wisdom, and the weakness of God is stronger than human strength.

1 CORINTHIANS 1:24–25 NIV

Blaze of Praise

♥♥♥♥♥♥♥♥♥♥

Your prayers are what give our Father God an opening to work His way in your life. The energy you send up to Him and the passion you display show Him how urgent each of your requests for His intercession are. Your words need not be perfect. Your meaning need not be totally clear. God knows what you need before you ask Him. He understands how you are feeling—and why. He longingly and lovingly wants to have a relationship with you, and prayer is the wonderful way of communicating with Him.

So go to your secret place. In that refuge, quiet your mind, heart, spirit, and soul. Then begin with identifying—for God and yourself—the amazing and absolute holiness of the One to whom you are praying. Follow with words asking Him to reveal Himself and His ways in your life. Tell Him that

you are prepared and want Him to do things here on earth as they are in heaven. Acknowledge that from His hand and His alone you receive your sustenance. That you are ready—and willing—to forgive others as He has forgiven you. Request that He keep you from the devil's wiles and ways. And, in a blaze of praise, acknowledge that He, God, is the Supreme Being, with all the power, beauty, glory, and honor in His name. So be it! So be you with God!

♥ ♥ ♥ ♥ ♥ ♥ ♥ ♥ ♥

"In this manner, therefore, pray: Our Father in heaven, hallowed be Your name."
MATTHEW 6:9 NKJV

Open Eyes

♥♥♥♥♥♥♥♥♥

You are in dire straits. And before you know it, your vision seems unclear. In your panic, your mind betrays you. You are no longer sure of the invisible power, so much are your eyes filled with earthly circumstances and apprehensions. When you are in such a state, I am here to tell you, there is nothing to fear. What you see is not the end-all and do-all. There is more to the invisible and spiritual world than you could ever know in your earthly form. Be not afraid. The powers that are with you are so much more than what appears to be coming against you.

Go back to what you know of our Father, Me, and the Spirit. We have overcome all. We are with you, surrounding you. Open up the eyes of your heart and your spirit—and see the truth of the matter! Behold your Father God who can divide the seas and rivers, blind an entire army, and stop the sun and the moon. Behold your Brother Jesus who can raise the dead, heal the leper, calm the wind, and silence the sea. Behold the Holy Spirit who gifts prophets, priests, laypeople, and kings. Open your eyes and see the power of God surrounding you—within and without. Believe—and you will be saved!

♥ ♥ ♥ ♥ ♥ ♥ ♥ ♥ ♥

"Do not fear, for those who are with us are more than those who are with them."
And Elisha prayed, and said, "LORD, I pray, open his eyes that he may see." Then the LORD opened the eyes of the young man, and he saw. . . . The mountain was full of horses and chariots of fire.

2 KINGS 6:16–17 NKJV

Standing Still

♥ ♥ ♥ ♥ ♥ ♥ ♥ ♥ ♥ ♥

Someone you love has encountered a situation, a problem, an obstacle. You are not sure how to advise this person. All you can do is feel his or her pain, anguish, and fear. At first, you rack your brain trying to figure out a solution, but you are too close to the person and the issue. Your heart is in your throat, and you don't know where to turn. Then, having exhausted all your human efforts and still knowing no way to fix things and having no peace, you come to Me. You realize this is too much for you to bear. You find yourself on your knees, admitting that I am the only One who can help you and your loved one.

My ears ring with joy at your pleas—not because you are under duress but because you realized you needed to come to Me! I already know the situation but now know the degree to which you are making yourself available to receive My wisdom, hope, and comfort. As you unburden your heart and I take things on My own shoulders, you rise. All you need to do now is follow My direction, walk in My wisdom, and breathe in My peace. The fight is now Mine—and Mine alone. Your job? To stand still and witness the victory I will set before you.

♥♥♥♥♥♥♥♥♥

"You will not even need to fight.
Take your positions; then stand still and
watch the LORD's victory. He is with you. . . .
Do not be afraid or discouraged."
2 CHRONICLES 20:17 NLT

Think, Then Speak

♥♥♥♥♥♥♥♥♥

As a mother, sister, daughter, friend, wife, mother-in-law, coworker, aunt, or daughter-in-law, your life and words touch the hearts of many, including your own. The things you say aloud to others and yourself—even in jest—can have a lifelong effect on the hearers. That is why it is so important to think before you speak. To make sure your words are encouraging, true, praiseworthy, necessary, gentle, kind, and uplifting.

There is so much darkness in the world. Use your words—written and spoken—to build others up, not tear them down. If you are not sure what to say, say nothing. If you feel My prompting, pray for wisdom before you speak. In all situations, know this: the words that come out of your mouth will be a reflection of the influence your knowledge of Me has had on your life.

♥♥♥♥♥♥♥♥♥

No one can tame the tongue. It is restless and evil, full of deadly poison. Sometimes it praises our Lord and Father, and sometimes it curses those who have been made in the image of God. And so blessing and cursing come pouring out of the same mouth. Surely, my brothers and sisters, this is not right!

JAMES 3:8–10 NLT

Quietness and Confidence

❤❤❤❤❤❤❤❤❤

How many times will you seek to do things in your own power before coming to Me for help? How often will you find yourself stressed out because you've forgotten where your true strength comes from? Yes, you are human. But you also have the light of God within you. You need to feed that fire by spending time with Me and in My Word. So stop running hither and yon, looking for answers, joy, and purpose in earthly wisdom and material possessions. Take a few moments to rest in Me, to be recharged in My power, to regain your strength.

Only I can give you the peace you need. Only I can calm your heart within so you can face the world without. Only I can give you the confidence to accomplish all you have been created to do. Only I can give you the wisdom to live a heavenly life on earth. So slow your steps. Remember and revel in your complete dependence upon Me. Then, and only then, will true joy fill your heart and the flame of your spirit light up the darkness in this world.

♥♥♥♥♥♥♥♥♥

For thus said the Lord God, the Holy One of Israel: In returning [to Me] and resting [in Me] you shall be saved; in quietness and in [trusting] confidence shall be your strength.

ISAIAH 30:15 AMP

Safety Net

♥♥♥♥♥♥♥♥♥♥

I alone am the answer to your worries. I alone can give you true peace. When you are fraught with worries, come into My presence. Speak My healing words to soothe your heart and spirit. Continually repeat, "Jesus is with me. All is well."

I can help you—and your loved ones—in any situation. I can not only save you spiritually but keep you safe physically. You need run to no other place but My arms. I am your Shepherd, willing to carry you, to die for you, to lead you, to heal you. I stand between you and the evil, the wolves of this world. With My staff and My rod ready to guide and protect you, you can rest easy. This peace, this confidence that only I can give you cannot be bought. It is fully and freely given— from My heart to yours, from My Spirit to yours,

from My mind to yours, from My soul to yours. Expect nothing less in the hours between sunset and sunrise. Bask in My peace. Slumber in My presence. Take that great leap of faith, for I am your safety net, on earth and in heaven.

♥ ♥ ♥ ♥ ♥ ♥ ♥ ♥ ♥

In peace I will both lie down and sleep, for You, Lord, alone make me dwell in safety and confident trust.
PSALM 4:8 AMP

Rock of Ages

♥♥♥♥♥♥♥♥♥

You have run to a house of straw to save you when you could've had help from Me—the Rock of Ages. I have helped you out so many times before. What took you so long in coming to Me now? Had the world convinced you that you could only solve this problem with earthly logic? Woman—say it isn't so!

Remember that My eye is always on you. My truth is at your fingertips. My Word is already on your tongue—and written on your heart.

The world has got everything upside down! It is My wisdom—not man's—that can make the impossible possible. It is My arm that is never too short to pull you up out of a pit. It is My solution that is far above any thoughts or imaginings of humankind. Commit your ways and means to

My hands alone. Make Me your primary aid—
and you will be on the winning side.

♥♥♥♥♥♥♥♥♥♥

*"You asked GOD for help and he gave you the
victory. GOD is always on the alert, constantly
on the lookout for people who are totally
committed to him. You were foolish to go for
human help when you could have had
God's help. Now you're in trouble."*
2 CHRONICLES 16:8-9 MSG

Spirit of Power

♥♥♥♥♥♥♥♥♥♥

This world would have you be afraid of your own shadow. Fortunately, you are My sister. And as such, you understand that God has given you the courage and boldness you need to live the life you were born to live. So do not give in to the fear of growing old and of not having enough.

Do not cringe when the world tells you you are not living up to its standards of beauty, poise, and wealth. Simply smile and walk away from the temptation to believe the world's lies.

You are a daughter of God. He knows how many hairs are on your head. He cares about every breath you take and every vow you make. And I, your Brother, value you so much that I sacrificed My life to save yours. And now I am living inside of you, leading you in the way you are to go, giving you the resurrection power to do all that you are designed to do.

So do not shy away from the challenge. Instead, embrace it. And let God's awesome power lead you to be the best you were made to be.

♥ ♥ ♥ ♥ ♥ ♥ ♥ ♥ ♥

For God did not give us a spirit of timidity (of cowardice, of craven and cringing and fawning fear), but [He has given us a spirit] of power and of love and of calm and well-balanced mind and discipline and self-control.

2 TIMOTHY 1:7 AMP

Sweet Forgiveness

♥♥♥♥♥♥♥♥♥♥

What is wonderful and humbling about forgiveness is not just giving it—but asking for it. When you come to Me, your heart in your hand, asking My forgiveness, it touches My heart, deep down. For in this desire for forgiveness, in this act of humility, you are closest to My Father's Spirit.

It is the same feeling that a mother gets when her child humbly comes into her presence, eyes down on the ground, feet shuffling, and tells her he broke her favorite china cup. Her tears cannot help but well up in her eyes as the mother sees the sincere remorsefulness and sorrow in her son's face. And as the years pass, wouldn't it be a wonderful lesson for him if she herself humbly asks him for forgiveness when she does him a wrong?

Forgiveness is sweet. And if it can be granted

by our Father to you all the years of your life, you shall be able to grant it to all those who wrong you—even if it takes 490 times.

♥♥♥♥♥♥♥♥♥

Then Peter came to Him and said, "Lord, how often shall my brother sin against me, and I forgive him? Up to seven times?" Jesus said to him, "I do not say to you, up to seven times, but up to seventy times seven."

MATTHEW 18:21–22 NKJV

Like a Child

♥ ♥ ♥ ♥ ♥ ♥ ♥ ♥ ♥

Where is the joyful innocence you once had? Where have the easy spirit, the trusting nature, the curious mind, the happy exuberance, and the enthusiasm gone? Do not let this world's shadows overcome your light. Do not let its wisdom drown out your spiritual intuition and discernment. Do not let its dog-eat-dog and it's-all-about-me attitude sweep you up in its embrace.

Instead, go against the worldly current by riding in the boat with Me. There will be times of storm, when the winds and the waves threaten to capsize your vessel. But with Me in the boat, you will never sink down into the depths but will walk on the water and someday rise up to paradise to be with Me. Heaven is the only true kingdom to aspire to, for it will still be there when all the

earthly kingdoms fall away.

So live this life with Me in joy! Trust and keep on trusting. Forgive and be forgiven. Love and be loved. Laugh, love, leap—and sing to the Lord a new song, the one you've kept hidden in your childlike heart.

♥♥♥♥♥♥♥♥♥♥

[Jesus] said, Truly I say to you, unless you repent (change, turn about) and become like little children [trusting, lowly, loving, forgiving], you can never enter the kingdom of heaven [at all]. Whoever will humble himself therefore and become like this little child [trusting, lowly, loving, forgiving] is greatest in the kingdom of heaven.

MATTHEW 18:3-4 AMP

Right Paths

♥ ♥ ♥ ♥ ♥ ♥ ♥ ♥ ♥

How much do you trust Me? With your life—or just your soul?

I trusted you with My entire being. I saved you even before you were formed in the womb. So why not trust Me now? If you have a decision to make or a problem that needs solving, My ears are ready and willing to hear all about it. There is no need for you to try to go it alone. Simply come to Me, and trust Me with all your heart—and mind!

As the Son of God, I have so much more wisdom that you can tap into—at any time and in any place. I am only a whisper of a prayer away. "Jesus, help!" is a prayer I constantly answer for those I love. So come to Me. Seek My wisdom. Listen for My voice in every situation you en-counter. Recognize Me for who I am. And I

will not fail to keep you on the right path and walking forward in supernatural confidence.

♥♥♥♥♥♥♥♥♥

Lean on, trust in, and be confident in the Lord with all your heart and mind and do not rely on your own insight or understanding. In all your ways know, recognize, and acknowledge Him, and He will direct and make straight and plain your paths.

PROVERBS 3:5–6 AMP

A Woman Aglow

❤ ❤ ❤ ❤ ❤ ❤ ❤ ❤ ❤ ❤

The world you live in seems to be growing some-
what darker. But that need not be any concern
of yours. For the darker the world, the longer its
shadows, the brighter My light becomes in you.

So do not abide in the shadows of this world.
Do not conform to the image of today's woman.
You are a daughter of the King. You already out-
shine all the jewels on earth. Your heart and mind
are aglow with the wisdom and knowledge of the
God who resides within you. You do not need
the trappings of this world to emit your beauty.
So keep your mind transformed and renewed
each and every day by keeping close to Me and
My Word. If you feel yourself slipping under the
shadow, enticed by the trappings of the world,
dragged down to its level, simply remind yourself,

"My mind is on God alone. He is all I need." In so doing, you will not only become all He has purposed you to be—but become the *best* you can be.

♥ ♥ ♥ ♥ ♥ ♥ ♥ ♥ ♥

*Do not be conformed to this world (this age),
[fashioned after and adapted to its external,
superficial customs], but be transformed
(changed) by the [entire] renewal of your mind
[by its new ideals and its new attitude], so that
you may prove [for yourselves] what is the good
and acceptable and perfect will of God,
even the thing which is good and acceptable
and perfect [in His sight for you].*

ROMANS 12:2 AMP

A New Challenge

♥ ♥ ♥ ♥ ♥ ♥ ♥ ♥ ♥ ♥

You are ready for a new challenge but unsure about your next step. Take your time. Look for My direction. Listen for My voice. You have stepped out before—and can do it again. Simply remember that each transition is a new beginning. That there is nothing you need to be afraid of when you are walking in the path I have laid out for you.

If there is ever any doubt, seek Me in prayer. Know that I am with you every step of the way. If you stumble, I will quickly grab your hand and balance you so that you can regain your foothold. Continually rise to new challenges. Stretch yourself so that you can become all God has created you to be. Never doubt your footing. Never fear humankind. After all—you're in My

hands. Nothing can truly harm you. Then, when you arrive at your new destination, learn all that you can. Be My light in that corner of the world by loving all you meet. Become an expression of Me, an extension of My compassion. Spread the word and change the world.

♥♥♥♥♥♥♥♥♥♥

Stalwart walks in step with GOD; his path blazed by GOD, he's happy. If he stumbles, he's not down for long; GOD has a grip on his hand.
PSALM 37:23–24 MSG

Seek the Lord

♥ ♥ ♥ ♥ ♥ ♥ ♥ ♥ ♥

Why do you continue to attempt things in your own power? Why do you not reach out to and rely on Father God in every aspect of your life? It's not that you should not seek out physicians to aid in healing your body. Nor should you not seek out advice from pastors, friends, family members, fellow believers, coworkers, or spouses. There are many who have the gift of healing, wisdom, helps, prophecy, discernment—and more! But they are merely mortal. They are not the best and last authority on any matter. They are not the God of all creation who knows every thought, feeling, and facet of your personality. They cannot divine what is truly in your soul or what path God has laid out for you. There is only one way to find the true power and path. And that is to come to Me. I will bring you to the Father. I will clear the obstacles out of your way. Seek the Lord your God; rely on Him alone. He will make all your paths straight. He will heal you, body, spirit, and soul.

♥♥♥♥♥♥♥♥♥

In the thirty-ninth year of his reign Asa was diseased in his feet—until his disease became very severe; yet in his disease he did not seek the Lord, but relied on the physicians.

2 CHRONICLES 16:12 AMP

Re-creation Powers

♥ ♥ ♥ ♥ ♥ ♥ ♥ ♥ ♥

When I was put in the tomb, My followers thought that was the end. But it was just the beginning! By the power of God, I was restored to life—and what a life! In this new body, I could walk through walls and appear seemingly out of nowhere! Those who were not sure of My resurrection and restorative powers could actually physically touch Me—and be truly and totally convinced that it was Me and that I had, indeed, risen from the dead.

My death, which seemed to make things appear so hopeless, gives you the best chance for your own re-creation. Know that God has a plan for you. Understand that He is determined to make you what you were designed to be. He has a vision for your life that cannot be deterred or obscured. Through each and every experience you are being re-created and strengthened until you become the ultimate you.

💜 💜 💜 💜 💜 💜 💜 💜

And after you have suffered a little while, the God of all grace [Who imparts all blessing and favor], Who has called you to His [own] eternal glory in Christ Jesus, will Himself complete and make you what you ought to be, establish and ground you securely, and strengthen, and settle you.

1 PETER 5:10 AMP

Humbly at Peace

♥ ♥ ♥ ♥ ♥ ♥ ♥ ♥ ♥ ♥

To become all that God has designed you to be, you must not let pride come between you and Him. For when you do, when you puff yourself up, you become more in love with the vision of who you think you are than the vision of who God may want you to be.

So be modest in every aspect of your life; after all, it is God who has created your mind, body, spirit, and soul. Your intelligence, appearance, heart, and personality were all formed by Him—with no help from you. Allow Him to have full control. Fill your mind with His Word. Treat your body as His temple. Align your spirit and soul under His direction. And when the moment is right, He will promote you to a seat of honor. Meanwhile, allow no bad news or concerns to

disturb the peace you find in Him. Take all your focus off what has or has not happened and put it on what God has been doing and will continue to do through you to make this world a better place—for you and all the women to follow your path.

♥ ♥ ♥ ♥ ♥ ♥ ♥ ♥ ♥

So humble yourselves under the mighty power of God, and at the right time he will lift you up in honor. Give all your worries and cares to God, for he cares about you.

1 PETER 5:6–7 NLT

Eyes Open

♥♥♥♥♥♥♥♥♥♥

While God is working out His renovation of you, be sure to keep strong in your faith. Keep your eyes open to any snares set up by the evil one. He may tempt you into believing that God has had no hand in your life. You have gotten where you are because of your own intelligence, looks, ability, personality, and spirit. Although it is fair to say that you have had some hand in your development, it's only because of your obedience to God, your belief in Me, and the help of the Holy Spirit that you are who you are and where you are today.

Because of your humble attitude, God has given you all the love and the grace you need to become the woman you are destined to be. So, as with all My other brothers and sisters, some who have suffered more, some who have suffered less

than you yourself, know that you are not in this alone. You have fellow sojourners who have been called to embark upon the same journey with the ultimate goal of sharing in the eternal glory through Me, your Christ.

♥ ♥ ♥ ♥ ♥ ♥ ♥ ♥ ♥

Stay alert! Watch out for your great enemy, the devil. He prowls around like a roaring lion, looking for someone to devour. Stand firm against him, and be strong in your faith. Remember that your Christian brothers and sisters all over the world are going through the same kind of suffering you are.

1 PETER 5:8–9 NLT

Power of Intentions

♥♥♥♥♥♥♥♥♥

Intentions are very powerful things. When you set an intention and then act upon it, amazing things happen. But even more amazing is that Father God can take whatever intention you have and make it work according to His plan—not only for you but for everyone else in your world. You see, *He* is the one with the ultimate power.

So no matter what comes against you, employ the power of rejoicing, of praising, of giving all cares up to God. Disregard whatever bad intentions others may have against you—their curses, their discouragements, their insults. Allow disparagements to simply roll off your back. Such things will harm the wrongdoers so much more than they will ever harm you—if ever! Instead, all those things will work together not only to accomplish God's will to help others, but to lift you to a higher, loftier place. And in that place, you can't help but be fearless, understanding, calm, forgiving, and totally content. After all, it's up to God to avenge any wrongs. You are simply here as an instrument of His good hand.

♥♥♥♥♥♥♥♥♥

Joseph said to them, "Don't be afraid. Am I in the place of God? You intended to harm me, but God intended it for good to accomplish what is now being done, the saving of many lives. So then, don't be afraid. I will provide for you and your children."

GENESIS 50:19–21 NIV

God Only Knows

♥♥♥♥♥♥♥♥♥

Why must you strain yourself, racking your brain, trying to figure out all the whys of life? Instead, rest in the knowledge that there are some things that only Father God knows. He has the entire plan in His hands. He is working things out for the good of one and all. He, through Me, is calling all believers to a trusting faith—to a place of peace within them. It is He who will make the dead to rise again upon My return. He is working His way through every detail, through the works of every being.

So rest easy. Be assured that God has all the answers, which are good and true. You need only respond to His call, to join Him in this great work. You need only follow the great commandments— to love God with all your heart, soul, strength, and mind. And to love others as you love yourself. So relax. Rest. Trust. Be at peace within and without. And most of all, love everyone—rich and poor, young and old, kind and cruel, ruler and laborer, believer and nonbeliever, giver and taker. And leave the rest to God, who knows all.

♥♥♥♥♥♥♥♥♥

GOD's Spirit took me up and set me down in the middle of an open plain strewn with bones. . . . He said to me, "Son of man, can these bones live?" I said, "Master GOD, only you know that."

EZEKIEL 37:1, 3 MSG

129

No More Fetters

♥♥♥♥♥♥♥♥♥

You are a woman with amazing opportunities. When you take your eyes off the ground and look up with a God perspective, there is nothing you cannot do. Hope in God. Wait for His timing. Expect good things to happen. Instead of seeing yourself as a limited being, cut away the fetters of your mind. Break the chain that binds you to self-limiting beliefs.

You have My resurrection power. You have God's strength and protection. You have the Holy Spirit's wisdom and direction. Soar as you were divinely designed to do. Rise above pride, pettiness, selfishness, self-absorption, greed, narrow-mindedness, and fear. Break away from the comfort of the ordinary and seek out a new world, the one God is calling you to. And as

you rise, as you mount up to the sun, you will find God becoming clearer and clearer. In His strength, you will not grow tired but find each updraft taking you higher and higher into His will. Wait. Expect. Change. And mount up. In His power, you will soar.

♥ ♥ ♥ ♥ ♥ ♥ ♥ ♥ ♥

Those who wait for the Lord [who expect, look for, and hope in Him] shall change and renew their strength and power; they shall lift their wings and mount up [close to God] as eagles [mount up to the sun]; they shall run and not be weary, they shall walk and not faint or become tired.

ISAIAH 40:31 AMP

Your Remedy

♥ ♥ ♥ ♥ ♥ ♥ ♥ ♥ ♥

You are in despair. Uncertain of ever finding a remedy for your pain. You have exhausted all your earthly resources—but you have never exhausted Me. Helpless, feeling lost in the crowd, you may have given up hope. But you have forgotten to trust in Me. Then one day, you quietly separate from the mass of bodies around you. As you emerge from the shadows, an eternal light breaks through to your thoughts. With a sudden revelation, you say to yourself, *There is one last chance for me. Perhaps—no, not perhaps! Something is telling me that, yes, He can save me! He is my remedy.* Quietly, almost fearfully, you come up behind Me and touch the fringe of My robe. I can feel the virtue, the power, the healing energy going out of Me and into you. In that instant, in that quiet space of light, in that eternal moment, you are healed. What took you so long?

♥♥♥♥♥♥♥♥♥

Daughter, your faith (your trust and confidence in Me, springing from faith in God) has restored you to health. Go in (into) peace and be continually healed and freed from your [distressing bodily] disease.

MARK 5:34 AMP

Amazing Praise

♥♥♥♥♥♥♥♥♥♥

When you face trouble, praise. When you are filled with fear, praise. When you are threatened and are uncertain of what to do, praise. When you need help from Me and My Father, praise. When you are discouraged, praise. When you meet the enemy face-to-face, praise. Lift up your head, seek My face, look for My light, then praise My name in a very loud voice: "Give thanks to the Lord! His amazing love lasts forever! He is the First and the Last! He is unchangeable! He is undefeatable! With Him in my life, no man or woman can harm me."

With such a mind-set, such a statement emanating from your lips, you will have victory— such victory that you will not be able to carry all the blessings you gain at My hand. Such amazing

praise, such a firm assurance in Me and My promises, cannot help but result in triumph!

💜💜💜💜💜💜💜💜💜

As they began to sing and praise, the LORD set ambushes against the men of Ammon and Moab and Mount Seir who were invading Judah, and they were defeated.... So Jehoshaphat and his men went to carry off their plunder, and they found among them a great amount of equipment and clothing and also articles of value—more than they could take away.

2 CHRONICLES 20:22, 25 NIV

Continual Renewal

♥ ♥ ♥ ♥ ♥ ♥ ♥ ♥ ♥

Why are you down in the mouth? Look up! Bless Father God. He always has good in mind for you. Since the day you were separated from Him in Eden, He has worked to bring you closer and closer to Himself. For thousands of years, He has given His people victory. He has saved them from themselves. He has conquered armies, He has forgiven gross transgressions against Him, He has pardoned the seemingly unpardonable, and He has kept His promises. He even sacrificed Me so you could reside with Him forever.

So don't forget all God has done for you—and all He has planned for you. He will continually fill your life with good things—from the cradle to the grave. It's not an age thing—it's a God thing. He will continually be renewing your heart, soul,

body, spirit, and mind. Do not worry about what the flesh looks like. Focus on continuing to grow your spirit more and more into the likeness of Me, His precious Son. Come with Me and feel His power, His strength, His replenishing Spirit. Daughter of God, continue to rise up and meet Him with praise!

♥ ♥ ♥ ♥ ♥ ♥ ♥ ♥ ♥

Bless (affectionately, gratefully praise) the Lord, O my soul, and forget not [one of] all His benefits. . . . Who satisfies your mouth [your necessity and desire at your personal age and situation] with good so that your youth, renewed, is like the eagle's [strong, overcoming, soaring]!

Psalm 103:2, 5 AMP

The Crazy Law of Love

♥ ♥ ♥ ♥ ♥ ♥ ♥ ♥ ♥

Love is the spirit of all the laws of God. It is what He wants from you above all things. Love is a reflection of God—because God is love. Love is the reason I laid down My life for you. And it's what God wants in return. And not just a superficial love. God wants you to love Him with every breath of your being. He wants you to love Him with not just a small or single part of you—but with *all* your heart, *all* your soul, and *all* your mind. And not just a sometime love—but an all-day, everyday love—with no holds barred! That's the first part.

The second part goes along with it. God wants you to love all others as you love yourself. That means respecting yourself. Looking out for the good of your own soul—as well as the souls of

everyone else on earth—whether they have been good to you or not. He wants you to be a constant giver of love, whether or not that love is deserved. When you were not deserving, I, the Son of God, sacrificed My life for you. Does it not make sense that God would want you to love others, regardless of whether it is deserved? Now that's crazy—but that's love!

❤ ❤ ❤ ❤ ❤ ❤ ❤ ❤ ❤

" 'Love the Lord your God with all your passion and prayer and intelligence. . . . Love others as well as you love yourself.' These two commands are pegs; everything in God's Law and the Prophets hangs from them."

MATTHEW 22:37–40 MSG

Overflowing with Hope

♥♥♥♥♥♥♥♥♥

Do you want the peace that surpasses all understanding? Then empty yourself of all worldly angst and worry. Put all your trust in Me. I am the One who can give you that amazing calmness, the One who can help you to sleep peacefully in the midst of a boat-rocking storm. This wonderful peace is a precursor to all-encompassing joy. And this joy and peace leads to an overabundance of hope!

It's available through the power of the Helper I sent to you thousands of years ago. That same power has not abated. That power was available to miracle workers of old—and is still available to you today. The same amount. The same strength. And you are the vessel for that power. All you need to do is trust your God, reach out, believe in Him, and He will fill you to overflowing with hope—all you need to lead a victorious life in Me. My greatest desire for you is that you live this blessed life to the fullest. Are you ready to have your cup runneth over?

❤❤❤❤❤❤❤❤❤

May the God of hope fill you with all joy and peace as you trust in him, so that you may overflow with hope by the power of the Holy Spirit.

ROMANS 15:13 NIV

The Word

♥♥♥♥♥♥♥♥♥

In the beginning was God. And He spoke things into being. His utterance, His Word, was Me. I have been around since the very beginning of time. Through Me, the world was made. For nothing was made until God spoke it (through Me, the Word) into existence. And with the help of the Holy Spirit, I continue to make God's thoughts clear to you through the written Word—that Bible you have before you. The precious book you hold in your hands.

As you read that Word, study it, and apply it to your life, you find yourself drawing closer and closer to God. The Word in action makes you more and more like Me. This Word is power. This Word is truth. This Word is the answer to every question you have in life. Take it to heart,

for nothing is more precious, more powerful, and more perfect.

♥ ♥ ♥ ♥ ♥ ♥ ♥ ♥ ♥

In the beginning [before all time] was the Word (Christ), and the Word was with God, and the Word was God Himself. He was present originally with God. All things were made and came into existence through Him; and without Him was not even one thing made that has come into being.

JOHN 1:1–3 AMP

Purpose-Filled Promises

♥♥♥♥♥♥♥♥♥

The Bible is not full of empty promises. No! It is full of powerful words—words that have been sent to accomplish God's purpose on heaven and on earth. Everything that He has said, all that He and I have promised, has an effect on the spiritual and the physical world. Scripture is alive, able to do everything from defeating evil, spreading peace, melting hearts, dividing and uniting kingdoms, subduing enemies, and toppling terrorists to changing lives, making dreams a reality, producing prosperity, strengthening marriages, raising children, abating sorrow, and more. From things mighty to things small, God's Word, His promises, are packed with power. There is no detail too small but God's promises have it covered. From the slightest worry to the most life-altering challenge,

God's promises apply. And there is nothing so great that the Word cannot conquer. So search the Word. Find a promise to apply to your life. And witness the power and purpose of the words that have come forth from His mouth to man's ear to your heart.

♥♥♥♥♥♥♥♥♥

So shall My word be that goes forth out of My mouth: it shall not return to Me void [without producing any effect, useless], but it shall accomplish that which I please and purpose, and it shall prosper in the thing for which I sent it.

ISAIAH 55:11 AMP

Ready Help

♥♥♥♥♥♥♥♥♥♥

I know all that is going on in your life. So please, do not try to hide yourself away. Instead, bring all your shame and troubles to Me. I am so ready to lift you above all your sorrows. I, too, have lived in your world. I have felt the pain and affliction it can bring. But I have also experienced the world's joys and triumphs.

So let go of all the chains that keep you from coming to Me. Break through all the self-made barriers that would have you cower in the dark. Step out of that dungeon and into the light of My presence. Walk right up and take what I am ready to give you. I have more mercy, love, kindness, and strength than you could ever imagine. And there is no one I would rather help than you, no one I would rather lift up than you, and no

one I would rather love than you, for I see who you really are and who you are about to be.

♥ ♥ ♥ ♥ ♥ ♥ ♥ ♥ ♥

Now that we know what we have—Jesus, this great High Priest with ready access to God—let's not let it slip through our fingers. We don't have a priest who is out of touch with our reality. He's been through weakness and testing, experienced it all—all but the sin. So let's walk right up to him and get what he is so ready to give. Take the mercy, accept the help.

HEBREWS 4:14-16 MSG

Certain as the Dawn

♥♥♥♥♥♥♥♥♥♥

Each and every day, return to Me. Read My Word to understand Me. Recognize when My hand is shaping and molding your life. Look for Me in unexpected places—in the flowers that bloom, the snow that falls, the river that winds, and the breeze that caresses your cheek. See Me in the eyes of a child, the kiss of a loved one, the scent on the air, the sun on your face, the flight of a bird, the joy in your heart.

I am in and all around you, keeping you safe, whispering in your ear, shielding you from danger, leading you through the labyrinth of life. You will find no better guide or teacher than Me and My Word. Learn us. Know us. Appreciate and cherish us. For we are one and the same. We are unstoppable. Like the streams that change the face of the earth over time, I am the Living Water that is helping you to carve out a godly life—for you and the children after you. As One who never changes, I will always come to you, certain as the dawn.

♥♥♥♥♥♥♥♥♥

Come and let us return to the Lord. . . . Yes, let us know (recognize, be acquainted with, and understand) Him; let us be zealous to know the Lord [to appreciate, give heed to, and cherish Him]. His going forth is prepared and certain as the dawn, and He will come to us as the [heavy] rain, as the latter rain that waters the earth.

HOSEA 6:1, 3 AMP

149

To Serve with Love

♥♥♥♥♥♥♥♥♥

Dear sister, I ask you to follow My example. Serve others with love—whether they have asked you to or not. Will you do so? Do you do so? When I was with My disciples, I got down on My knees to wash their feet. In so doing, I hoped they would see how they were to serve each other— no questions asked. And to allow others to serve them—no questions asked.

So do not protest when those you feel are "above" you seek to serve you. Allow them to experience the joy of a servant's heart. Do not try to pay them back, but allow them to feel the selfless love they have given you. Then go and do the same for some other soul. Without being asked, serve with love, compassion, desire, humility, and grace. Such an act on your knees will raise your spirit high—in this world and the next.

♥ ♥ ♥ ♥ ♥ ♥ ♥ ♥ ♥

*"Now that I, your Lord and Teacher,
have washed your feet, you also should wash
one another's feet. I have set you an example
that you should do as I have done for you.
Very truly I tell you, no servant is greater than
his master, nor is a messenger greater than the
one who sent him. Now that you know these
things, you will be blessed if you do them."*

JOHN 13:14–17 NIV

Rise Up!

♥ ♥ ♥ ♥ ♥ ♥ ♥ ♥ ♥

Just when things look like they won't get any better, just when the cold and darkness seem to be swallowing you whole, remember Me. Come away with Me. Rise above the sorrows of this world. Like spring, I have come to warm your heart and lighten your load. In My presence, the winters of life hold no power—and the certainty of spring is on the rise. With Me, you can bloom where you are planted, no matter what the earthly season. You will hear the voice of the birds who live to sing praises in My name.

This is your season. This is your spring. This is your period of renewal, joy, warmth, and light. Let Me see your face, hear your voice. Know that when you are with Me, winter becomes a vague memory. So raise your arms and lift them up to the Son.

♥ ♥ ♥ ♥ ♥ ♥ ♥ ♥ ♥

My beloved spoke, and said to me: "Rise up, my love, my fair one, and come away. For lo, the winter is past, the rain is over and gone. The flowers appear on the earth; the time of singing has come, and the voice of the turtledove is heard in our land."

SONG OF SOLOMON 2:10–12 NKJV

Live, Laugh, Love

♥ ♥ ♥ ♥ ♥ ♥ ♥ ♥ ♥

Yes, there is trouble in your world—on the spiritual and material planes. But as I have told you before, "I have overcome the world!" So don't allow the doom and gloom to settle on your heart. Don't let each and every piece of bad news destroy your triumphant outlook. You are My followers—so rejoice! Even if you don't feel like smiling, smile anyway. And before you know it, it will be a continual habit.

Take some time out of each and every day to play, to lose yourself in the simple, easy things. In the privacy of your home, spin, twirl, skip. Before you know it, you will be laughing like a child. Such a lift will be a gift to your heart. Earthly life is too short to be weighed down by wars, murders, terrorists, fires, and all other calamities. You

were never meant to hear and bear the news of an
entire world—or even your own little piece of it.
So stop the madness. Live, laugh, love. It does a
body—and soul—good.

♥ ♥ ♥ ♥ ♥ ♥ ♥ ♥ ♥

A cheerful disposition is good for your health;
gloom and doom leave you bone-tired.
PROVERBS 17:22 MSG

On the Other Side

♥ ♥ ♥ ♥ ♥ ♥ ♥ ♥ ♥

I know the pain you are feeling. I, too, shed tears for those who passed on from one world to the next. But trust Me. You will see them again one day. After all, I have promised this to you. There is a place that I have set aside for each and every believer. So do not worry about them leaving you behind. They will be waiting for you on the other side. And when your time comes, you will be reunited with them— forever.

In the meantime, know that this hurt shall eventually fade away. Nothing can really ever separate you from the love you had for that person and the love she had for you. Hold the richness of that thought in your heart. And remember the mansion that awaits in the sky for the followers of God's light and Word.

♥ ♥ ♥ ♥ ♥ ♥ ♥ ♥ ♥

*"Don't let this throw you. You trust God,
don't you? Trust me. There is plenty of room
for you in my Father's home. If that weren't so,
would I have told you that I'm on my way to get
a room ready for you? And if I'm on my way to
get your room ready, I'll come back and get
you so you can live where I live."*

JOHN 14:1–3 MSG

157

Precious Lamb

♥♥♥♥♥♥♥♥♥

You are My precious lamb. There are so many things you have yet to discover, so many lessons you have yet to learn, so many paths you have yet to travel with Me. So follow closely. Spend much time in My presence. Then you will learn to know and recognize My voice when I speak. You will be familiar with My promptings, those sparks of divine intuition, inspiration, and ideas. There will be a wonderful connection between My Spirit and yours. You will more easily be led to where I am guiding you.

Yes, learn My voice—every word, inflection, tone, and correction. Do not lose the import of what I say to you. Become so familiar with My way, My light, and My spark that you will be able to know Me, your Shepherd, in the flash of an

eye and obey Me just as quickly, even when amid
a crowded flock.

♥ ♥ ♥ ♥ ♥ ♥ ♥ ♥ ♥

*"My sheep hear My voice, and I know them,
and they follow Me. And I give them eternal life,
and they shall never perish; neither shall anyone
snatch them out of My hand. My Father,
who has given them to Me, is greater than all;
and no one is able to snatch them out of My
Father's hand. I and My Father are one."*

JOHN 10:27–30 NKJV

God's Eyes

♥ ♥ ♥ ♥ ♥ ♥ ♥ ♥ ♥

Are you doing whatever you think is right in your own eyes? If so, what weights are you using on your scale of rightness and wrongness? What is your litmus test?

In the days of the judges, there were no kings in Israel. So everyone did what he thought was right—and chaos ensued. But you, dear sister, have a King in your life—He is God the Father. He is looking at what you are doing, discerning your true motive, and testing your heart. Is it in line with His will for your life? Have you determined if it meets the parameters of the great commandment—to love God, yourself, and others? If you are ever in doubt, stop. Come to Me. Ask Me to reveal your true intents, your heart, the purpose behind your actions. Ask Me to allow you to take a step back, to see things with God's perspective, to remove the scales from your eyes. Come outside of yourself to see within yourself and the truth that lies there. Then, once you are certain that your will is in line with God's, continue on with our blessings.

♥ ♥ ♥ ♥ ♥ ♥ ♥ ♥ ♥

We justify our actions by appearances;
God examines our motives.
PROVERBS 21:2 MSG

Magic Elixir

♥♥♥♥♥♥♥♥♥

In your world, your time in My presence is a
magic elixir for the soul. That calmness and contentment you gain is what keeps the spirit and
the bones healthy. Stop trying to get everything
under your control. Those efforts are futile—and
lead only to an early demise. Instead, acknowledge that you are grateful just going where I lead,
knowing that I will equip you for every task for
which I have given you an urging.

Quiet your soul as you come into My presence.
Like a baby who no longer needs milk from her
mother's breast, be happy where you are. Allow
your heart to be at peace. Let the pressures and
conflicts of this particular time in your life fade
away into nothing. Rest in My arms where there
is nothing but light and a gentleness beyond

compare. Let Me hold you, stroke your hair, whisper a lullaby. Rest, secure in Me. Then wait and hope, today and all the days to come.

♥ ♥ ♥ ♥ ♥ ♥ ♥ ♥ ♥

GOD, I'm not trying to rule the roost, I don't want to be king of the mountain. . . . I've kept my feet on the ground, I've cultivated a quiet heart. Like a baby content in its mother's arms, my soul is a baby content. Wait, Israel, for GOD. Wait with hope. Hope now; hope always!

PSALM 131:1–3 MSG

Perseverance

♥ ♥ ♥ ♥ ♥ ♥ ♥ ♥ ♥

You have come up against many obstacles in your efforts to complete an endeavor. You have suffered many trials. Come to Me for whatever extra energy and courage you need to finish the task at hand. Know that with My help, you can do anything. Know that I am working within you to help you bring things to completion. Never doubt for a second that this thing will be done.

You have the talent. You have the drive. You have the vision. You have the determination. You have the will. And I have given you the way. So do not despair but keep on keeping on. Persevere against all odds and you will be rewarded, for you have put feet to your faith. And that always makes Me smile, for it tends to make unbelievers gasp.

♥ ♥ ♥ ♥ ♥ ♥ ♥ ♥ ♥

It is profitable and fitting for you [now to complete the enterprise] which more than a year ago you not only began, but were the first to wish to do anything [about. . .]. So now finish doing it, that your [enthusiastic] readiness in desiring it may be equalled by your completion of it according to your ability and means.

2 CORINTHIANS 8:10–11 AMP

165

Heart's Desires

♥♥♥♥♥♥♥♥♥

What are the desires of your heart? To find your true love? To have children? Have a successful career? Serve others? Become a surgeon? Graduate from law school? Or are you uncertain as to which road to take in any of those life directions?

If you are not sure what your true desire is, come to Me as a young girl to her big brother. Sit next to Me and ask whatever questions you will. I will answer. Together we will discover your true desire. Perhaps it was a dream you gave up long ago. Perhaps it was a childhood wish that you never thought possible. Whatever it is, you will discover and obtain that which you were designed to be when you seek out and enjoy the presence of My Father and Me. All secrets will be revealed. All desires will be met. All dreams

will become reality. That is the work and will of My Father and Me. Come. Discover a new place, a new life, a new dream, a new way, a new joy with Us.

♥♥♥♥♥♥♥♥♥

Delight yourself also in the Lord,
and He will give you the desires
and secret petitions of your heart.
PSALM 37:4 AMP

Let Peace Reign

♥ ♥ ♥ ♥ ♥ ♥ ♥ ♥ ♥

Your heart is thumping. Tears begin to well up in your eyes. To hide the fact that your fists are clenching and unclenching, you fold your arms in front of your chest. When your teeth begin to clamp together, you realize that this is not the time to make a decision. That's the light from Me. That's My prompt, telling you to get while the getting is good. To extract yourself from the current situation. To come and seek My face.

If you allow Me, I will give you the peace you need before you speak. I will give you the wisdom you need to make the right decision, to help your heart and your mind come to the right conclusion. So, when your emotions threaten to take control, run—into My arms! Give Me your anger, your tears, your stress, your troubles. And I will help you give My peace the reins.

♥♥♥♥♥♥♥♥♥

*And let the peace (soul harmony which comes)
from Christ rule (act as umpire continually)
in your hearts [deciding and settling with
finality all questions that arise in your minds,
in that peaceful state] to which as [members of
Christ's] one body you were also called [to live].*

COLOSSIANS 3:15 AMP

169

Resurrection Power

♥♥♥♥♥♥♥♥♥♥

Do not worry about the power of temptation. Do not see the things that plague you as forces that cannot be overcome. Do not be concerned about the limited vision you have in certain areas of your life. Forget about all the issues, problems, and sometimes people, that seem to weigh you down. God sent Me to help you. He has given Me all the power I need to break you out of any spiritual, emotional, financial, physical, and mental prison you are in. He has given Me the healing power to restore your sight. He has given Me the strength to carry whatever burdens you are bearing. He has given Me the keenness of mind to deliver you from unhealthy relationships.

Simply come to Me, knowing that I, whom God raised from the trappings of death, am going

to change your life. I am going to raise you from whatever binds you. Trust in that resurrection power. . . . I am your example that anything is possible. Trust in Me.

♥ ♥ ♥ ♥ ♥ ♥ ♥ ♥ ♥

God's Spirit is on me; he's chosen me to preach the Message of good news to the poor, sent me to announce pardon to prisoners and recovery of sight to the blind, to set the burdened and battered free, to announce, "This is God's year to act!"

LUKE 4:18–19 MSG

Uplifting Praise

❤❤❤❤❤❤❤❤❤❤

Lift your arms in praise, like a tree stretching to meet Me in the sky. Open your arms wide to capture the blessings of sunshine, rain, and snow. Raise your face, basking in the glow of My light, the power of My words, the cleansing of My touch. Open your heart to the love I am ready to lavish upon you. Allow it to fill your entire being, leaving no corner untouched. Allow it to heal every disappointment, hurt, sorrow, and pain you have endured. Open up your soul to the truth I am waiting to set upon you. Allow it to expand your vision, until you see Me in every part of your life. Open up your spirit to hear My voice loud and clear. Allow it to change you from the inside out, making you more and more like Me. Lift your entire being up to our Father. Be glad in all

you are, in all that He has made you to be. Share the joy We bring to you, today and every day. Let not your heart ever be troubled. Let the sweetness of His name, His works, and His blessings overflow from His arms into yours.

♥ ♥ ♥ ♥ ♥ ♥ ♥ ♥ ♥

May the glory of the LORD endure forever; may the LORD rejoice in His works. . . . I will sing to the LORD as long as I live; I will sing praise to my God while I have my being. May my meditation be sweet to Him; I will be glad in the LORD.

PSALM 104:31, 33–34 NKJV

The Ultimate Weapon

♥ ♥ ♥ ♥ ♥ ♥ ♥ ♥ ♥

Thoughts are flitting through your mind all the time. They ricochet from one corner of your brain to another. Fortunately, you were not designed to follow every idea that comes into your head. If you did, you'd be going in a thousand different directions at once. That's because it's only the thoughts you claim that have the real power. And the more you own them, the longer you let them linger, the more powerful they get. Over time, these claimed thoughts grow feet, arms, and legs and take on a life of their own.

That is why you need to take all thoughts captive and bring them into My light. Test them against My Word. Realize that they are only thoughts, after all. Using My strength, My Word, you can regain control. The power you have in

Me—that is your ultimate weapon. That is how you can change your thoughts, which will in turn change your mind, your life, and the world.

♥ ♥ ♥ ♥ ♥ ♥ ♥ ♥ ♥

The weapons we fight with are not the weapons of the world. On the contrary, they have divine power to demolish strongholds. We demolish arguments and every pretension that sets itself up against the knowledge of God, and we take captive every thought to make it obedient to Christ.

2 CORINTHIANS 10:4–5 NIV

A Door Wide Open

♥♥♥♥♥♥♥♥♥

I am calling you to a new space, a new area, a new opportunity, a new endeavor where you will do mighty things. Are your ears open? Do you hear My voice? Are you ready to glorify God—or is something holding you back? Others initially refused their call. Moses didn't think he was a good enough speaker to talk for God. Jonah initially refused to tackle the mission Father God had for him—so he became bait and was swallowed by a large fish. Then there was Gideon, whom the angel of God addressed as a mighty warrior while he was still a farmer threshing grain.

Dare to believe that I am calling you. That although a new path may seem scary, it is the right path. That I will not send you out ill equipped. Break free from the fetters of your comfortable

world. Stop listening to the lies that you aren't good enough, smart enough, strong enough. You are a woman who, when she makes up her mind to, can accomplish anything with Me. I am holding the door wide open. Walk through to a new life.

♥♥♥♥♥♥♥♥♥

For a wide door of opportunity for effectual [service] has opened to me [there, a great and promising one], and [there are] many adversaries.

1 CORINTHIANS 16:9 AMP

Loved Ones

♥ ♥ ♥ ♥ ♥ ♥ ♥ ♥ ♥

I am here, ready and waiting. Bring your loved ones before Me. No words need be said. I can read your mind's desire for each one. I can discern your heart's concerns, pick up on your hopes, see your dreams, and feel your love for each one of them. They are precious in your sight—and Mine. Bring them before Me, and then let them go, one by one. Put them into My care and leave them here. Know that I will do what's best for them.

The love you show as a mother, wife, sister, aunt, grandmother, friend, and fellow believer warms My heart. And the faith that you have in Me, to leave all your worries and what-ifs in My capable hands, puts a smile on My face. Allow Me to hold this burden for you. You have done what you could. You have revealed the wonder and truth

of your faith. You are demonstrating both to those you love, and they will be the richer for it. May your faith continue to umpteen generations.

♥ ♥ ♥ ♥ ♥ ♥ ♥ ♥ ♥

That precious memory triggers another: your honest faith—and what a rich faith it is, handed down from your grandmother Lois to your mother Eunice, and now to you!

2 TIMOTHY 1:5 MSG

Heart Dreams

♥ ♥ ♥ ♥ ♥ ♥ ♥ ♥ ♥

What are the dreams you hold in your heart, in that secret place deep, deep down where you commit your most precious thoughts? Tell Me, tell Me all. I want to know what you yearn for. I want to hear what path you would like to take in My name. I want to understand what you are thinking, how much you trust Me, how willing you are to just take things day by day.

I am here to remind you to honor your dreams that I have planted in your heart. They are there for a reason—because you are the only one who can live that dream. A space in time has been carved out for you. Are you willing to seek it, to fill the void no one else can? Honor your dreams. Make a space for them in your life. And then, when you find your path, when you

are completely satisfied to take what I give you day to day and then trust Me—and only Me—for the rest, amazing things will begin to happen. Follow your dreams. Then once you are on your road, help to honor the dreams of others. Help them realize their goals—and glorify Me!

💜 💜 💜 💜 💜 💜 💜 💜

May He grant you according to your heart's desire and fulfill all your plans. . . . Some trust in and boast of chariots and some of horses, but we will trust in and boast of the name of the Lord our God.

PSALM 20:4, 7 AMP

Time of Testing

As I was tested in the Garden of Gethsemane, so you will have times of testing in your own life. Do not worry about these seasons, for I will always be there to help you bear up under them, as Father God helped Me. I even asked Him if He would take the cup from Me. But He did not. And after the pain and torture, I ended up saving the world, rising again in God's amazing power.

You, too, can request help and clarity from God—but know that if a time of trial is God's will and way, He will give you the help to bear up under it. He will give you the strength to do what He has given you to do. And you, too, will see the amazing joy and victory when your testing is over. For you will have learned how to endure, how to ride the wave with God through every tempest and storm.

♥ ♥ ♥ ♥ ♥ ♥ ♥ ♥ ♥

*Dear. . .sisters, when troubles come your way,
consider it an opportunity for great joy.
For you know that when your faith is tested,
your endurance has a chance to grow. So let it
grow, for when your endurance is fully developed,
you will be perfect and complete, needing nothing.*

JAMES 1:2–4 NLT

Shallow-End Advice

♥ ♥ ♥ ♥ ♥ ♥ ♥ ♥ ♥

Time and time again, Father God and I have saved you from your enemies—seen and unseen. We have kept you from being snared by the evil one. We have given you a way out when you were faced by temptation. We put a hedge of protection around you when you begged for Us to shield you from harm. In these times of danger, you breathed the words, "Jesus, help me!" and I immediately responded. Afterward, your heart still pounding, you were praising Us over and over again. Yet the next day you'd forgotten all about what We had done for you! Sister, may this not be so!

Remember our promises! Remember how often We have saved you from yourself and others. Keep all these rescues in mind once you are safe. But do not become complacent. And above all, don't run

headlong into another sticky situation. Stop! Wait! Ask for My help before your next move. Call on Me while you're still in the shallow end—not ready to jump off the high dive. Stop. Wait. Ask. Then follow our advice. Remember our promises. Then you will praise our name!

♥ ♥ ♥ ♥ ♥ ♥ ♥ ♥

[The LORD] rescued them from their enemies. . . .
Then his people believed his promises.
Then they sang his praise. Yet how quickly they
forgot what he had done! They wouldn't wait for
his counsel! In the wilderness their desires ran wild,
testing God's patience in that dry wasteland.

PSALM 106:10, 12–14 NLT

Pouring Out

♥ ♥ ♥ ♥ ♥ ♥ ♥ ♥ ♥

Tell Me all that is on your mind. Hold nothing back! Pour your heart and soul out to Me. Let your armor drop. Let your guard down. Allow nothing to stand between us—no weapon, no shield, no shame. Enough of the brave front, the facade, the mask that you wear in front of so many others. Show Me the true you. I will not turn you away. I will not mock you. Instead, I want to know you. I crave to know exactly what is going on in your life.

There is no need for you to sugarcoat anything. Believe Me—I have heard it all, so nothing you say is going to shock Me. Let's talk together. Let's get it all down to the bare bones so we can build your life up again. There is no need to fear Me. Simply come. Talk. And pour out your soul. I am here to receive all that you say, all that you are, all that you have been—and help fill you up again.

♥ ♥ ♥ ♥ ♥ ♥ ♥ ♥ ♥ ♥

*Hannah answered and said, "No, my lord,
I am a woman of sorrowful spirit. I have drunk
neither wine nor intoxicating drink, but have
poured out my soul before the LORD. Do not
consider your maidservant a wicked woman,
for out of the abundance of my complaint
and grief I have spoken until now."*

1 SAMUEL 1:15–16 NKJV

Remember Lot's Wife

♥♥♥♥♥♥♥♥♥

How willing are you to follow Me? What are you willing to leave behind on the material plane to become closer to Me on the spiritual plane? How much are you willing to sacrifice so you can truly move forward?

Each and every day you have a choice to make—to come with Me down the path I have laid out for you or to stay where you are, no matter what the consequences. It's all up to you. If you disregard My pleas and stay on the plane of your current existence, you may just end up stuck there, wondering where your opportunity went. But if you decide to listen to Me, to follow My lead, you will find yourself going forward to the mountain, continually rising up higher and higher, closer and closer to God and the kingdom of heaven.

Perhaps you may start out with Me but then,

longing for what had been, look back at what you've left behind. Chances are, that constant looking back will bring not only discontentment but more trouble in the long run. So decide. What are you going to do—walk with Me, eyes looking forward, or look back at your own peril?

♥ ♥ ♥ ♥ ♥ ♥ ♥ ♥

And when they had brought them forth, they said, Escape for your life! Do not look behind you or stop anywhere in the whole valley; escape to the mountains [of Moab], lest you be consumed. . . . But [Lot's] wife looked back from behind him, and she became a pillar of salt.

GENESIS 19:17, 26 AMP

God Space

♥♥♥♥♥♥♥♥♥

The diaper pile seems to be growing by the moment. Your new job is asking for more responsibility— but offering less pay. You're not sure you've got anything to cook for dinner tonight, but you're too tired to stop at the store. The weekend you had planned to get away has been canceled—due to your having to nurse a sick husband. There seems to be no time, no energy, no you left.

I, too, had My fill of work thousands of years ago. My days were spent preaching, teaching, healing, and blessing one person after another. But I knew how to recharge. I would walk away from the crowds and find My own space to be alone with God our Father—many more times than the Bible notes. Where do you go to get re-fueled by God? Where do you go to regain your strength, compassion, energy, and love? Carve out your own wilderness in life. Make a space that will be occupied by you and God—alone. Then take off your mask. Come face-to-face with your Maker. Pray for His touch of healing, love, and guidance. Rest as long as need be. But come. Don't delay.

♥ ♥ ♥ ♥ ♥ ♥ ♥ ♥ ♥

Despite Jesus' instructions, the report of his power spread even faster, and vast crowds came to hear him preach and to be healed of their diseases. But Jesus often withdrew to the wilderness for prayer.

LUKE 5:15–16 NLT

Born to Abide

♥♥♥♥♥♥♥♥♥

Without Me, you can do nothing. There is nothing you can do in your own power. That is why I am here. That is why I was sent to save you. I am your link to the life of abundant joy, love, peace, and provision. So follow Me. Live a life of love. Maintain a heart for the one and only God of the heavens. Believe that we are with you every step of the way. Stay close, so close you can no longer see where we begin and you end. Stay close enough that you can hear My breathing, feel My chest rise and fall, see My shadow right alongside your own.

Imprint My words upon your mind. Apply the Bible to your life. Seek My wisdom, My face, My smile. Think with your heart of flesh—not the cold reasoning of the mind. Believe that love is the greatest power on earth. Know that when you are abiding in Me, whatever you ask Me, I will do for you. Stop living alone. Stay with Me.

♥ ♥ ♥ ♥ ♥ ♥ ♥ ♥ ♥

Dwell in Me, and I will dwell in you. . . .
If you live in Me [abide vitally united to Me]
and My words remain in you and continue
to live in your hearts, ask whatever you will,
and it shall be done for you.

JOHN 15:4, 7 AMP

Heavenly Exchange

♥ ♥ ♥ ♥ ♥ ♥ ♥ ♥ ♥

Money is not everything. Neither are material possessions or good looks. The kind of car you drive doesn't matter, either. In fact, it doesn't even matter if you *own* a car. None of these things matter because they will neither get you into heaven nor help you to experience the kingdom of God here on earth. What *does* matter is your forgetting about yourself and what you want. What matters is your clinging so tightly to Me that you don't see anyone—or anything—else. Because when it's all said and done, you will only be saved by giving up your life for Me—as I have done for you.

All that is required, then, is for you to put Me first in this life. You are to follow My example by walking in My footsteps, loving and forgiving others regardless of whether they love and forgive

you. So stop the petty quarreling, the striving after money, the bitterness held in the heart, the competition for material goods. Drop all at My feet. Then pick up My cross and follow Me. It's a heavenly exchange.

♥♥♥♥♥♥♥♥♥

Jesus said to His disciples, "If anyone desires to come after Me, let him deny himself, and take up his cross, and follow Me. . . . For what profit is it to a man if he gains the whole world, and loses his own soul? Or what will a man give in exchange for his soul?"
MATTHEW 16:24, 26 NKJV

Eagles' Wings

♥♥♥♥♥♥♥♥♥

I have seen what you've been up to. I have you constantly in My sights. In fact, I travel to and fro over the face of the earth to keep an eye on all My people. My message to you today is to not despair. There will be times when your plans go awry. When you come against too many obstacles. When you come to a fork in the road and are just not sure of which path to take. All of this is part of the journey. All of this is what keeps drawing you back to Me. All of this is what will make you stronger so you can sense My presence, look for My hand, and seek My voice.

You are My special girl. You are My extraordinary possession. I have been, am, and remain only a sigh away. Call Me. Speak to Me. Ask Me whatever you will. I am here for you. As in times past, I will carry you on eagles' wings and bring you back to Me. So go. Obey. Love. And above all, do not despair. I am here to swoop you up at any point in time.

♥ ♥ ♥ ♥ ♥ ♥ ♥ ♥ ♥

"You have seen what I did to Egypt and how I carried you on eagles' wings and brought you to me. If you will listen obediently to what I say and keep my covenant, out of all peoples you'll be my special treasure."

EXODUS 19:4–5 MSG

Adventure Afoot

♥ ♥ ♥ ♥ ♥ ♥ ♥ ♥ ♥

The alarm goes off. You roll out of bed. Your feet hit the floor, and you stagger off to begin your day. You may spend a second, a minute, a half hour in prayer. And then you are caught up in the happenings on the material plane, the physicality of your own little world. You find yourself unhappy and/or a bit frustrated with life as you sit in traffic, change the 351st diaper, see someone else get "your" raise, or find that first gray hair. In the midst of all this chaos, one can find herself forgetting that she is not alone. That there is a bigger and better adventure afoot. That there is an entirely different perspective on this life.

When you see things with My eyes, when you acknowledge and keep yourself aware of the amazing power that is abiding in you, you find your life becoming one you'd never considered. It is beyond your hopes and dreams. It is the life in Christ—and that makes all the difference in heaven and on earth.

♥♥♥♥♥♥♥♥♥

Now to Him Who, by (in consequence of) the [action of His] power that is at work within us, is able to [carry out His purpose and] do superabundantly, far over and above all that we [dare] ask or think [infinitely beyond our highest prayers, desires, thoughts, hopes, or dreams]—to Him be glory.

EPHESIANS 3:20–21 AMP

The Poison of Bitterness

♥ ♥ ♥ ♥ ♥ ♥ ♥ ♥ ♥

He said, she said. If only you would remember what *I* have said. I know how hard it can be to be betrayed. I know the pain of vindictiveness. I know what it is like to have people reject you, slander you, and desert you. Yet in spite of all those things I suffered, I never once cursed God or the people of the earth. So why should you?

Forget about getting even with those who betrayed, hurt, and slandered you. Instead, forgive them. Forget about the ones who deserted you. If you are not on their mind, why should they be on yours? Do not let bitterness and strife poison you and those around you. Forget about the feuds. Leave all rancor behind—instead come to Me. I will help you find the forgiveness you need. Cry on My shoulder. Let it all out, and then let it all

go. Life is too short to allow bitterness to weigh you down. So let it roll off. Let it lie at My feet. Then rise up and feel the weightlessness of your new being. And if someday you find the thing returning, simply come to Me again and again until it weighs less and less and finally disappears altogether.

♥♥♥♥♥♥♥♥♥

Look after each other so that none of you
fails to receive the grace of God. Watch
out that no poisonous root of bitterness grows
up to trouble you, corrupting many.
HEBREWS 12:15 NLT

Net Works

♥ ♥ ♥ ♥ ♥ ♥ ♥ ♥ ♥

I am looking for team players. I am looking for women who are willing to follow My direction, no matter how futile it seems. I see what you have been up against. I understand what you have been trying to do. I know you are exhausted, tired of not getting ahead, of putting your line out there and not getting any bites. You feel as if you are working so hard but getting nowhere fast.

Relax. Listen to My voice. Heed My direction. As I helped Simon Peter, I am going to help you. I will do My part, but you need to do yours. Once I give you My direction, you need to follow it—no matter how illogical it sounds! For I am using God's wisdom, which at times seems foolish to humankind. In exchange for this utter confidence in Me, you will find yourself obtaining

so many fish in your once-empty net that your boat will be in jeopardy of sinking! You will be bewildered and amazed. You will be blessed beyond belief, which will draw you more and more irresistibly to Me! So break out the nets! Let's go fishing together!

❤ ❤ ❤ ❤ ❤ ❤ ❤ ❤ ❤

*Simon answered and said to Him,
"Master, we have toiled all night and caught
nothing; nevertheless at Your word I will let
down the net." And when they had done this,
they caught a great number of fish,
and their net was breaking.*

LUKE 5:5–6 NKJV

203

The Promises Foretold

♥ ♥ ♥ ♥ ♥ ♥ ♥ ♥ ♥

You are a mighty woman. You are an amazing creature, built to accomplish amazing things. You are brave, determined, loving, kind, gentle, joyful, patient, promising, faithful, humble, worthy of sacrifice, and more! "But," you may say, "these things are not true of me. They are things that I want to be, that I strive for. But I am so far away from being the creature You want me to be—and now say that I already am!" Yet that's just what faith is.

I am telling you things that, in My eyes, already exist. That is how I see you—as a woman complete in every way, shape, and form. I am not restricted or limited by time. I can see who you are about to become. So keep the faith. Understand the promises. You have a God who can grow a life inside a ninety-year-old woman!

Do not place limits on a God who will not and cannot be chained down! What He has promised you has, in His eyes, already come through. So, sister, simply have faith! And all that is written about your new life in Christ will be—or actually, already is!

♥ ♥ ♥ ♥ ♥ ♥ ♥ ♥ ♥

As it is written, I have made you the father of many nations. [He was appointed our father] in the sight of God in Whom he believed, Who gives life to the dead and speaks of the nonexistent things that [He has foretold and promised] as if they [already] existed.

Romans 4:17 AMP

Wind beneath Your Wings

❤❤❤❤❤❤❤❤❤

You have been wishing, waiting, hoping, and praying for your desire to be met. And you have hung in there, shown your perseverance. Even when you felt you couldn't go on, when you felt as if your heart just couldn't take it anymore, you stuck with it. You refused to be discouraged. And now your hopes have borne fruit! Your desire has been met! Your goal obtained! Suddenly you have wind beneath your wings. You are ready to soar!

This is the day to sing praises to the Lord—to let the world know that with Me, anything is possible! When you line up your goals with what God wants for your life, there is nothing you cannot do. Now take a few moments to imagine what it will be like when you, My follower, come into the kingdom of heaven. What a day of glory

that will be! What a wonderful new life you will begin! No more pain, no more sorrow, no more disappointment. You will finally be back in the garden, in paradise. There all desires will be met. There you will see Me face-to-face. There will all your dreams—and Mine—be fulfilled, forever and ever, amen!

♥ ♥ ♥ ♥ ♥ ♥ ♥ ♥ ♥

Hope deferred makes the heart sick,
but a longing fulfilled is a tree of life.
PROVERBS 13:12 NIV

No Problem Too Small

♥♥♥♥♥♥♥♥♥♥

I am interested in every detail of your life. There is no problem too small, no discouragement too vague, no grievance so slight that I am not concerned about it. I have told you before how important you are to Me. So when you come to Me, do not hide anything. Do not let the slightest problem furrow your brow. Let it all out. When you do, your heart will feel lighter. Your creases will ease. Your anger will dissipate, your sorrow will turn to joy, your worries will be sent packing, your disappointments will fade away, your shame will lessen, and your frustrations will be eased. What once frightened you will diminish when put into words, brought into My light, and left at the foot of My cross. All this weight that you carry will slough off of your shoulders and onto

Mine. So come. Bring Me your all. Drop it at My feet. And when you are ready, leave My presence as light, airy, and free as a little sparrow.

❤❤❤❤❤❤❤❤❤❤

"Are not two sparrows sold for a penny? Yet not one of them will fall to the ground outside your Father's care. And even the very hairs of your head are all numbered. So don't be afraid; you are worth more than many sparrows."

MATTHEW 10:29–31 NIV

Continuous Spring

♥♥♥♥♥♥♥♥♥

I am your Living Water. When you trust and believe in Me, when you rely on Me like no other, when you take a drink of the water I can give you, your entire life will change. My water will begin a work like no other. It will give you inner strength and courage, inner wisdom and clarity. You will be overflowing with an abundant supply of everything you need to face the outer world. People will come to you to be refreshed, for you are not a stagnant being but an ever-flowing river of hope, love, faith, and charity.

All that you need, I am. All that you can be, I can sustain. All that you desire will be met and satisfied by My ever-flowing, ever-abundant living water. You need not strain any longer but simply believe, trust, and rely on the Word that I

have spoken, the Word that changes lives forevermore, the Word that gives you an endless supply of love and water for life, to forever change your inner world and therefore the outer world.

♥ ♥ ♥ ♥ ♥ ♥ ♥ ♥ ♥ ♥

Whoever takes a drink of the water that I will give him shall never, no never, be thirsty any more. But the water that I will give him shall become a spring of water welling up (flowing, bubbling) [continually] within him unto (into, for) eternal life.

JOHN 4:14 AMP

Walk in the New

❤ ❤ ❤ ❤ ❤ ❤ ❤ ❤ ❤

Only when you believe things with your entire mind and whole heart will you understand Me. Only then will My identity, My purpose become clear. Only then will My presence be revealed. You need to dig down deep into the heart of the entire matter and see that, although thinking of My suffering may bring you down, you can and shall be filled with joy—because I have done as the prophets predicted! I have died, risen again, and so overcome the world.

Don't let your intellect get in the way of My saving grace. Don't let the Gospel story become so well known that the mystery is taken for granted and its power supplanted by passivity. Allow Me and My joy of having saved you reign in your heart above all. Search for Me in the Old

Testament—but walk with Me in the New. Keep your eyes upon Me and My Word in your heart. Together we will see the kingdom of God come into your life—after which neither you nor the world will ever be the same.

♥ ♥ ♥ ♥ ♥ ♥ ♥ ♥ ♥

Then he said to them, "So thick-headed!
So slow-hearted! Why can't you simply believe
all that the prophets said? Don't you see that
these things had to happen, that the Messiah
had to suffer and only then enter into his glory?"

LUKE 24:25–26 MSG

Holy Spirit

♥ ♥ ♥ ♥ ♥ ♥ ♥ ♥ ♥ ♥

After My resurrection, when I met My two disciples on the road to Emmaus, I saw how confused they were as to My power and My purpose. They didn't clearly understand how I had fulfilled the scriptures. So I opened their minds so that they could comprehend everything that had happened. But you, and all the rest of My followers, have another Helper. His name is the Holy Spirit. When you became a believer in Me, you were clothed with His power. There is nothing He does not understand about Me and the Father. There is no question He cannot answer. But it first has to be asked.

Pray for the Holy Spirit's wisdom. Pray for His guidance. Even if you stumble in trying to frame a question, He'll get it. He'll bring it to

Me and the Father. And together We will make things known to you. Together all meaning will become clear. Together We will open up the scriptures, your heart, and your mind. Stay in the Word, forever learning and growing in wisdom and empowered from on high.

♥♥♥♥♥♥♥♥♥

He [thoroughly] opened up their minds to understand the Scriptures. . . . And behold, I will send forth upon you what My Father has promised; but remain in the city [Jerusalem] until you are clothed with power from on high.

LUKE 24:45, 49 AMP

215

The True Path

♥ ♥ ♥ ♥ ♥ ♥ ♥ ♥ ♥

Time and time again I am longing to give you direction. But oftentimes you don't ask. Forget about worldly wisdom. Because it's based on the wisdom of fellow humans, it's oftentimes fallible. But My promptings to you, My direction when heeded will keep you on the straight and narrow path. So don't follow the world's way. Don't try to fit in with society or follow your flesh. Be your own woman with a godly mind-set.

The Holy Spirit is always at your beck and call, and I reside within you. Plus Father God is only a prayer, a sigh, a breath away. So come to us for each and every decision—large and small. Test it against God's Word. Look for My face when you are in prayer. Continue seeking God's kingdom, and you will find yourself on the right road,

for it is God who knows when you may need to make a detour. It's He who knows where the big potholes of trouble lie. It is He who knows what bridges are out. Seek out Our spiritual guidance, and you will find your way home.

♥♥♥♥♥♥♥♥♥

Don't fool yourself. Don't think that you can be wise merely by being up-to-date with the times. Be God's fool—that's the path to true wisdom. What the world calls smart, God calls stupid. It's written in Scripture, He exposes the chicanery of the chic. The Master sees through the smoke screens of the know-it-alls.

1 CORINTHIANS 3:18–20 MSG

Childlike Wonder

♥ ♥ ♥ ♥ ♥ ♥ ♥ ♥ ♥

After spending time in My presence, go out with a sense of wonder. Know that I can do amazing and powerful things, things you can't even imagine. I have ideas for your life that you could never think possible—but I am the Lord of impossibilities. Look for Me to amaze you. Expect the unexpected blessings.

Look for Me around every corner, and you will find Me. Maintain that mind-set, that joy of expectancy all day. Recognize Me moving in your life. Praise and thank God for every blessing bestowed upon you. I am the Lord of miracles. I am the Lord who can give you unsurpassed peace. I can raise people from the dead, heal the lame, turn water into wine, calm the sea, and still the wind. With a wave of My hand, a nod of My

head, a whisper to My Father's ear, the world is forever changed. Live with a childlike wonder, curious as to what I will do next. In doing so, you will be living a joy-filled life.

♥ ♥ ♥ ♥ ♥ ♥ ♥ ♥ ♥

And overwhelming astonishment and ecstasy seized them all, and they recognized and praised and thanked God; and they were filled with and controlled by reverential fear and kept saying, We have seen wonderful and strange and incredible and unthinkable things today!

LUKE 5:26 AMP

Angels with You

♥ ♥ ♥ ♥ ♥ ♥ ♥ ♥ ♥

I am sending angels with you, to help prosper you on your journey. Feel their presence surrounding you. They will help you, keep you from tripping on the path, stumbling over a stone. They will give you protection, as they did for Daniel when he was in the lions' den. They will rescue you, as they did for Lot when they saved him from fire and brimstone, and as they freed Peter when he was trapped in prison. Because you are constantly and consistently walking in My presence, I have cleared the road before you. And you will have success—because it is My plan for your life. It is My life that is abiding in you.

Keep close. Don't deviate. Keep praying at every turn and fork in the road. Wait for My promptings when necessary. Believe Me, I have

the timing down. Trust Me in all things and your mission will be achieved! Success at last! In the end you will give credit where credit is due—not to angels but to Father God. For He is the Lord of all. He is the master planner. He is the One who is deserving of your praises.

♥ ♥ ♥ ♥ ♥ ♥ ♥ ♥ ♥

"He [Abraham] responded, 'The LORD, in whose presence I have lived, will send his angel with you and will make your mission successful. Yes, you must find a wife for my son from among my relatives, from my father's family.' "
GENESIS 24:40 NLT

Heart Prayers

♥♥♥♥♥♥♥♥♥♥

I know exactly what you need and when you need it. I know the thoughts of all people, including you and those around you. For Me, there are no surprises. Before you are even done praying, before the words have left your lips, an answer is on its way. There can be no delay. Know this as a fact. Live this in your life. Be assured that there is not one thing I do not know. Understand that all My knowledge is too much for you. And that there is a reason you don't know or have all the answers. That's what this faith thing is all about.

To be saved from the world of humankind and your own self, you must have complete faith and trust that I am here. I know all. I am listening to your prayers. I am always moving and putting things in place for your good.

I am always working in your life because your life is precious to Me. And nothing on heaven or earth can separate you from My love. So come. Pray. And I will move in your life for good.

♥♥♥♥♥♥♥♥♥

"Before I had finished praying in my heart, I saw Rebekah coming out with her water jug on her shoulder. She went down to the spring and drew water."

GENESIS 24:45 NLT

Continue On!

♥♥♥♥♥♥♥♥♥

When your dreams and prayers are answered, when what you desired has come about, what then? Continue on! Don't slow down! Keep up your momentum. There may be more to your mission than you thought. So stay on your trek. Take the good word back to the people you serve. Come to Me, and thank Me for My help. Allow nothing to hinder you. For if you take too much time to stop and congratulate yourself, to celebrate with people who had nothing to do with your efforts, your message may not get through after all. And your momentary success may turn into a disaster. Yes, you may rest and refresh yourself for a little while, but remember, it is all in My timing.

So take all your trophies, all you have earned

with My help, all the blessings you have received, and come back to Me, your Master. Tell Me all about your excursion. And when you have reached your destination, make yourself ready to go out again, with hope, love, and good news on your lips.

♥♥♥♥♥♥♥♥♥

He said, "Oh, don't make me wait!
GOD has worked everything out so
well—send me off to my master."
GENESIS 24:56 MSG

Mighty Warrior

❤❤❤❤❤❤❤❤❤❤

I see things in you that you have no idea you possess. I see you as brave, determined, loving, kind, gentle, and simply amazing. You see, I know what you are equipped for. Every moment, hour, day, month, year, you are becoming more and more of what God created you to be. You may be saying to yourself, "Why, I'm no one special. Just an ordinary career woman, mother, wife, daughter, sister, friend, artist, or believer." But woman, you are so much more. You are mighty in courage and love. You have untold power that I have given you, beyond what you could ever dream of. There is so much more to you than meets the eye—and most of it lies within. I am here to awaken your courage. To draw you unto Me. To convince you that you can do whatever you set your mind to.

That the strength you already have is what you are going to draw on wherever I send you. When you are living in My power, when you are allowing Me to work through you, when you take Me with you every step of the way, you are not just any woman. You are a mighty warrior.

♥ ♥ ♥ ♥ ♥ ♥ ♥ ♥ ♥ ♥

One day the angel of GOD came and sat down under the oak in Ophrah that belonged to Joash the Abiezrite, whose son Gideon was threshing wheat in the winepress. . . .
The angel of GOD appeared to him and said, "GOD is with you, O mighty warrior!"

JUDGES 6:11–12 MSG

Complete in Spirit

♥♥♥♥♥♥♥♥♥♥

Slow down. Stand still. In these moments, rest
with Me. Breathe easy. Relax your jaw. Unclench
your fists. Let your shoulders drop. Allow your
body to soften. You are safe here in this space,
in My presence. So let all tension dissolve. Focus
on Me. My peace. My love. My desire to fill you
with light, promise, and hope. Allow no corner of
your heart, body, soul, mind, and spirit to remain
in the shadows. I am in Father God. You are in
Me. And I am in you. Together we are complete,
one in spirit.

Rest here. Allow My thoughts, promises,
and words to fill your mind. You are alive in
Me because you have faith in Me and who I
am. You are not like the nonbelievers who are
like sleepwalkers in this world, going through

the motions day after day and never finding the God who can save them, love them, touch them, bring them to life. But you are here with Me now, learning more and more about Me and the Father. Linger here longer each day, until you reach the point where you can access Me and My power at and in any moment.

♥ ♥ ♥ ♥ ♥ ♥ ♥ ♥ ♥

"In just a little while the world will no longer see me, but you're going to see me because I am alive and you're about to come alive. At that moment you will know absolutely that I'm in my Father, and you're in me, and I'm in you."

JOHN 14:19–20 MSG

Rise Up

♥ ♥ ♥ ♥ ♥ ♥ ♥ ♥ ♥

The world has a way of beating people down. Of causing the innocent to suffer. Although God's law is written on the heart of every person, that does not mean he or she follows it. But I am here to walk with you. I am here to remind you that all is not lost. For you have found God. You may be weary, trying to make a living, raising children, keeping house, teaching at church, and supporting your community. You want to be the representation of Me and My love to all you meet. But you are growing tired. Your hands are weakening. You feel like you are swimming against a wicked current.

Take courage. I am going to right all the wrongs that have been done. I am walking alongside you. I have overcome the world—and because I am in you, you, too, will see victory. So take a while to rest up. And then rise up again.

Stand still and straight. Focus. Be brave, knowing that you will triumph in the end. Continue the good work. With Me on your side, you cannot lose.

♥ ♥ ♥ ♥ ♥ ♥ ♥ ♥ ♥

Energize the limp hands, strengthen the rubbery knees. Tell fearful souls, "Courage! Take heart! GOD is here, right here, on his way to put things right and redress all wrongs. He's on his way! He'll save you!"
ISAIAH 35:3–4 MSG

Forever Prayers

♥ ♥ ♥ ♥ ♥ ♥ ♥ ♥ ♥

The world is full of hurting people, believers and nonbelievers alike. Some are hurting because of the choices others have made. Some are hurting because of their own choices. Regardless of the cause, one thing remains: people who need someone to stand in the breach for them. People who need much prayer. Whether it is sickness, injury, addiction, murder, theft, idolatry, or the reaping of what they have sown that is coming against them, people need an intercessor. Who can you stand in the breach for today? Who can you help save with your prayers? Who can you give a fighting chance to?

You are one of God's chosen few. You have an intimate relationship with Me and the Father. Your prayers can change the world, one person at a time. So who is it today? Who can you bring before Us? Perhaps you, too, were once separated from God. Perhaps someone once stood in the breach for you. When you are taken from the earth, the power of the prayer lives on and on, from one generation to the next. Who can you pray a forever prayer for today?

♥♥♥♥♥♥♥♥♥

God their Savior. . .said He would destroy them. [And He would have done so] had not Moses, His chosen one, stepped into the breach before Him to turn away His threatening wrath.

PSALM 106:21, 23 AMP

Jesus on Board

♥ ♥ ♥ ♥ ♥ ♥ ♥ ♥ ♥ ♥

Things started out pretty calmly. You were going your own way, minding your own business, when all of a sudden things started going wrong. The wind started howling, the waves grew bigger. Your life was being rocked back and forth. You were struggling to hold on, to stay above the water. Then you imagined a demon heading your way. Now you're even more terrified because not only is the natural world working against you, but so is the supernatural.

But relax! It's only Me. I am here to help, to save, to boost your courage. Let Me on board. Let Me be a part of your life. Trust Me to help—not hinder. Trust Me to equip you for all you need to reach your goal—not to get you off course. Trust Me to steer you in the right direction—not lead

you astray. Trust Me to keep your head above water—not weigh you down. Just trust Me. And before you know it, you'll be exactly where you were heading to in no time.

♥♥♥♥♥♥♥♥♥

They were maybe three or four miles out when they saw Jesus walking on the sea, quite near the boat. They were scared senseless, but he reassured them, "It's me. It's all right. Don't be afraid." So they took him on board. In no time they reached land—the exact spot they were headed to.

JOHN 6:20–21 MSG

Follow the Spirit

♥ ♥ ♥ ♥ ♥ ♥ ♥ ♥ ♥

It may be hard to believe, but you are a stranger in this world. This earth, this planet is not your primary residence. You were made for the Garden of Eden, and it is for this reason I was sent. It is for this reason that I was sacrificed, so you could return to your true land, your true place, your true relationship with God.

I am your tie to paradise. I am your way in. You know the path. You know that you are to love God with all your being and to love your neighbors as you love yourself. You know you are to abide in Me, as I abide in you. You know that without Me you can do nothing, go nowhere. Follow the urgings of the Spirit within you, not the flesh. Keep your eyes, your focus, on Me. I will lead you to the true Promised Land—a life with God in the New Jerusalem. Stay much in My company and you will find your way to your true home. As it was in the beginning. . .

♥ ♥ ♥ ♥ ♥ ♥ ♥ ♥ ♥

The land shall not be sold into perpetual ownership, for the land is Mine; you are [only] strangers and temporary residents with Me. . . . Beloved, I implore you as aliens and strangers and exiles [in this world] to abstain from the sensual urges (the evil desires, the passions of the flesh, your lower nature) that wage war against the soul.

LEVITICUS 25:23; 1 PETER 2:11 AMP

237

Milk and Honey

❤❤❤❤❤❤❤❤❤❤

You need not be afraid of anything. No matter what you face, I will fight for you. There is no foe who can withstand My power. There is no giant I cannot slay. So why fear the monsters built up in your imagination? Why talk yourself out of getting in the water without even wading in up to your ankles?

Woman, you are more than flesh and blood. You are spirit—and when you abide in Me, I am abiding in you. There is no foe we cannot face together. So do not lose courage just when you are on the edge of entering the Promised Land. For if you do, you may spend more time in the wilderness than you want to. Instead, delight in Me. Seek My face, courage, heart for battle. I will give you everything you need to vanquish every fear and foe—imaginary or not. Do not shrink back to the old land, where you were enslaved by temptation, fear, and angst. Stop murmuring. Pick up your spiritual armor and go forward with My name on your lips, God's power in your soul, and the Holy Spirit's strength to conquer all. This land is yours.

♥ ♥ ♥ ♥ ♥ ♥ ♥ ♥ ♥

"If the LORD delights in us, then He will bring us into this land and give it to us, 'a land which flows with milk and honey.' Only do not rebel against the LORD, nor fear the people of the land, for they are our bread; their protection has departed from them, and the LORD is with us. Do not fear them."

NUMBERS 14:8–9 NKJV

The Name Jesus

♥♥♥♥♥♥♥♥♥

The power of My name—Jesus. There is no other name with such authority. To those who are walking in darkness, Jesus brings light. To those who are groping the walls as if they were blind, Jesus provides direction, a new road, a new life. To those who are trembling, Jesus brings strength. To those who are weak kneed, Jesus brings courage. To those who are unprotected and unsheltered, Jesus provides a shield and a home. To those who are ill of body, mind, spirit, and soul, Jesus heals. And the key to unleashing all this power to the individual is faith—faith that I am the light that will lead you out of darkness. That I am the One who can give you a new vision. That I am the One who can strengthen, protect, shield, and heal.

Yes, I am the One with the power, but you are the one who must have the belief to apply that power to your life and see it live in every aspect of your being. It is only My power combined with your belief in Me and My name that will make you whole.

♥ ♥ ♥ ♥ ♥ ♥ ♥ ♥ ♥

"Let it be known to you all, and to all the people of Israel, that by the name of Jesus Christ of Nazareth, whom you crucified, whom God raised from the dead, by Him this man stands here before you whole."

ACTS 4:10 NKJV

The World Shifts

♥♥♥♥♥♥♥♥♥

I have seen you down on your knees, knowing
what has driven you there: your love for another.
Whether it be a child, a man, a friend, a relative,
your love for that individual has fueled your prayer
like nothing else ever can. For in those moments,
you are totally focused. I see what you see clearly.
I feel what you feel, down to the very last pang. I
have not driven you to this. You have approached
Me in this fashion. And it tells Me more than you
can imagine. It tells Me your true heart's desire.
And to this I cannot help but respond—not just
by answering your prayer, but by lifting you to
your feet. And it is in this exchange, your reaching
out for My help, stretching out your arms in love,
seeking Me and My face above all else, that I,
too, most readily reach out across the seeming

void, stretching My arms and extending My love, seeking you and your tender face, your mother's tears, your daughter's cries, your husband's pain, your friend's ache. And when we touch, when our very beings become united as one, the world shifts.

♥ ♥ ♥ ♥ ♥ ♥ ♥ ♥ ♥

The Lord God is my Strength, my personal bravery, and my invincible army; He makes my feet like hinds' feet and will make me to walk [not to stand still in terror, but to walk] and make [spiritual] progress upon my high places [of trouble, suffering, or responsibility]!

HABAKKUK 3:19 AMP

Your Compass

In the beginning, Father God spoke. And what He spoke was the Word. Scripture is a vast wonderland to be explored. Each story, each poem, each chapter of history contains infinite lessons. There is no end to the knowledge and wisdom that lie therein. Study it. Meditate upon it. Drench yourself in it. How else will you learn to know My voice? How else will you find My comfort, light, love, heartbeat? How else will you know what path to take? How else will you grow into the woman God wants you to be?

It all awaits you there—from Genesis to Revelation. The world may scoff, but it does not know the treasures of the Word. It does not understand the hope, power, love, understanding, and miracles that lie within. Read the Word. It's meat for

your bones. It's light for your way. It's the compass for your path.

♥♥♥♥♥♥♥♥♥

*Even if it was written in Scripture long ago,
you can be sure it's written for us. God wants
the combination of his steady, constant calling
and warm, personal counsel in Scripture to
come to characterize us, keeping us alert
for whatever he will do next.*

ROMANS 15:4 MSG

Remember Me

♥♥♥♥♥♥♥♥♥♥

When you have been swallowed by trouble, I am there. When the waves are breaking over your head and you are gasping for air, I am waiting for you to turn to Me, to reach out, to say My name. When you feel as if you cannot escape the current, I am ready to rescue. When you feel the slick seaweed pulling you deeper and deeper, when you think you are too entangled to ever escape, when you feel you will never find a foothold, My arms are reaching out, My soles are dug deep, and I am waiting. . .for you to remember Me. And when you do, I am spurred into action. When you think no one can hear your cry, your voice comes to My ear. And I answer your call. From the deepest, darkest recesses, I bring you into the light. I lift you above the waves, out of the current, up from the seaweed. You are Mine. Remember Me.

♥♥♥♥♥♥♥♥♥

"The engulfing waters threatened me,
the deep surrounded me; seaweed was
wrapped around my head. To the roots of the
mountains I sank down; the earth beneath
barred me in forever. But you, LORD my God,
brought my life up from the pit."

JONAH 2:5–6 NIV

Transition to Transformation

♥♥♥♥♥♥♥♥♥♥

One day My followers saw Me totally transformed, as white as white can be. Someday you, too, will be transformed, to a new life after your bodily death. In the twinkling of an eye, you will rise from the ashes. Your mortal body shall be made immortal. You will meet up with Me in heaven! Oh, what a day that shall be. For I have triumphed over death. And because you believe in Me, you, too, shall be victorious. You will be forever free from the bodily restraints that kept you captive. So do not fear physical death. It has no hold over you. And there will be other saints, all together, singing praises over and over to the Holy One who sits on the throne.

I have been with you from the beginning. And I will be with you at the end. When it comes

time for your physical death, do not be afraid. I will still have you in My capable hands. With Me, you need not fear transition—but glory in transformation! Simply continue to believe—and it will be.

♥ ♥ ♥ ♥ ♥ ♥ ♥ ♥ ♥

We'll all be changed. In the resurrection scheme of things, this has to happen: everything perishable taken off the shelves and replaced by the imperishable, this mortal replaced by the immortal. Then the saying will come true: Death swallowed by triumphant Life! Who got the last word, oh, Death? Oh, Death, who's afraid of you now?

1 CORINTHIANS 15:52–55 MSG

Lay It Down

♥ ♥ ♥ ♥ ♥ ♥ ♥ ♥ ♥

I have laid down My life for you. There is no greater friend you could ever have, no greater love you can ever possess. So what makes you think I will not be there for you in each and every situation you ever encounter? Heartbreak, fear, challenge, sickness, death, terror. . . I am with you. I always have been. I always will be. So dry those tears. Banish those fears. Rise above your illness. Snap your fingers at the threat of death. Turn away from terror. None of these things hold any power over Me—or you. Lo, I am with you until the end of the age—and beyond.

And because I am with you, because you need not fear anything, because I have laid down My life for yours, you are to lay down your life by doing for others as I have done for you. For how can you

gorge yourself on cake when you have a brother dying of hunger? Or how can you buy a new dress if you have a sister who has no clothes on her back? How will others understand the love of God if you, a woman of His Way, do not help others in obvious need? I am with you—and you will be doing My work if you are there for them. Lay your life down, sister. Lay it down, and you will rise up with Me.

♥♥♥♥♥♥♥♥♥

This is how we know what love is: Jesus Christ laid down his life for us. And we ought to lay down our lives for our brothers and sisters.

1 JOHN 3:16 NIV

Deep to Deep

♥♥♥♥♥♥♥♥♥♥

I became flesh—Me, the Word. I once walked among you in bodily form. I, with skin and bones, blood and marrow, walked the earth you now walk, breathed the air you now breathe. I was once a physical part of your world. And part of My chemical makeup will always be among you, as the earth is constantly recycling the old and the new. Yet spiritually I am still all over the earth. From the north to the south, the east to the west, I am in your midst. You see, feel, hear, and know Me when your deep calls to My deep. When your spirit calls to Mine. And I rush through time and space to be at your side.

I always have been, forever am, and always will be. And there is not one week, day, hour, minute, second that goes by that I do not think

of you. Walk with Me—day and night. Let the world scoff. It knows nothing of our reality. Take My hand. Come with Me, and you will never walk alone.

♥♥♥♥♥♥♥♥♥

[Roaring] deep calls to [roaring] deep at the thunder of Your waterspouts; all Your breakers and Your rolling waves have gone over me. Yet the Lord will command His loving-kindness in the daytime, and in the night His song shall be with me, a prayer to the God of my life.

PSALM 42:7–8 AMP

Write the Vision

I have given you a specific task, something that only you and you alone can do. Are you doing it? Are you investing your talents? Are you trying again and again, continually persevering? Or have you given up on your dream, the vision for your life?

Don't you know that this task I have asked you to do and your dream are one and the same? It's true! There is a talent within you. Do not fear to cultivate it, to grow it, to use it. For it's all according to My plan, My will, My path for you. And do not think you have to risk everything to be what I have called you to be. When need be, stop. Wait for it. Then take one step in some way toward your dream. And then, little by little, you will attain your goal; you will get to where I want you to be.

So begin your dream by honing your talent. Then take one little step after another. Before you know it, you will be a few feet down the road, closer to your destiny, closer to Me. So get out there. Live your story. After all, a book is not written in one day but begins with a pen, some paper, and one letter at a time.

♥ ♥ ♥ ♥ ♥ ♥ ♥ ♥ ♥

"Write the vision and make it plain on tablets, that he may run who reads it. For the vision is yet for an appointed time; but at the end it will speak, and it will not lie. Though it tarries, wait for it; because it will surely come, it will not tarry."

HABAKKUK 2:2–3 NKJV

A Melt Through

♥♥♥♥♥♥♥♥♥

There are harsh, cruel, cold people in the world. But there are also people like you—soft, gentle, and kind—who can help those on the dark side. For nothing melts a heart more than a kind word, gesture, or smile. Practice that kind of loving attitude, and you will melt some of the ice around the edges of another's heart. It does not matter if you see no visible change in that person. Nor does it matter if others mock you for being so gentle and sweet—to the good and the not so good. The mockers themselves may not know of the kind of love you silently "speak." But never mind. Someday the cold ones and the mockers will begin to understand the language of your love. Someday they will crave more and more of your goodness. And little by little, you will win them over to Me.

And that's not just a breakthrough—that's a melt through.

♥♥♥♥♥♥♥♥♥

God makes a huge dome for the sun—a superdome! The morning sun's a new husband leaping from his honeymoon bed, the daybreaking sun an athlete racing to the tape. That's how God's Word vaults across the skies from sunrise to sunset, melting ice, scorching deserts, warming hearts to faith.

PSALM 19:4-6 MSG

The Other Side

♥ ♥ ♥ ♥ ♥ ♥ ♥ ♥ ♥

You have lost a precious loved one. Cry on My shoulder. Give Me all your grief. Do not try to maintain a "stiff upper lip." Let it all out. Your tears do not reveal weakness but compassion. Just as I was overwhelmed with compassion when I saw My people lost and without a shepherd, I have compassion upon you. Just as I wept when I learned Lazarus was dead, I weep with you. Together we will bear up under this load of compassion and care. Together we will show our love to the heartless and hopeless in this world. And as we do so, they will turn to Me. They will understand that being Christian does not mean no longer having pain—but having compassion for ourselves and others as we go through that pain. It also means seeing our ultimate hope—

everlasting life for all believers—on the other side. Hold on to that hope. It's a matter of life—not death.

♥♥♥♥♥♥♥♥♥

Jesus told her, "I am the resurrection and the life. Anyone who believes in me will live, even after dying. Everyone who lives in me and believes in me will never ever die. Do you believe this, Martha?"
JOHN 11:25–26 NLT

Touching the Untouchable

♥♥♥♥♥♥♥♥♥

Never hesitate to approach Me. Never think that your sins are so great that you cannot face Me. Never believe that I am too busy to tend to you, that you could ever be a bother. Never imagine that your faith is so little that I cannot use you. Allow nothing to hinder your coming.

Remember the leper who approached Me? In that day, he was considered an "untouchable." Yet he broke through the crowds. He humbled himself before Me. He worshipped Me, no holds barred, and then demonstrated his faith by saying, "Lord, if you want to, you can not only heal me but make me clean." What courage! What belief! Of course I was willing! I then touched the untouchable leper—and healed him. Instantly, he was cured and cleansed! Do you need curing? Do

you need cleansing? Do you have courage? Come to Me. Do not hesitate. Do not let other seekers crowd you out. Do not let mockers steer you away. Do not let your state of mind, body, or spirit trip you up. Come. No matter how untouchable you feel, I will touch your life and make you whole once more.

♥ ♥ ♥ ♥ ♥ ♥ ♥ ♥ ♥

Jesus reached out and touched him.
"I am willing," he said. "Be healed!"
And instantly the leprosy disappeared.
MATTHEW 8:3 NLT

Love on the Journey

♥♥♥♥♥♥♥♥♥♥

You lie in bed, wondering where all the years have gone. What happened to all your dreams? The goals you set for yourself? All the things you were going to achieve? How did you get so far off your preset course? Life happened. Those unexpected events, obligations, roadblocks. But were they really?

What you may have considered an obstacle became an opportunity to show My love. What seemed like an obligation became a test of faith. What appeared as an unexpected event was actually planned by Me all along. So be patient, My sister, with yourself and others. See all things as a gift from our Father, as an opportunity to show the world My hands, feet, voice, light, laughter, and love. Yes, continue to dream dreams—and

strive to achieve them. Yet understand that it's all about revealing My love on the journey and not the destination itself.

♥♥♥♥♥♥♥♥♥♥

Sisters, we urge you to warn those who are lazy. Encourage those who are timid. Take tender care of those who are weak. Be patient with everyone. See that no one pays back evil for evil, but always try to do good to each other and to all people.

1 THESSALONIANS 5:14–15 NLT

Go Deep

♥♥♥♥♥♥♥♥♥

Many times I walked off alone, went into the mountains to be with Father God. In His presence I prayed the night away. All this was to prepare Me for the decisions and doing of His will the next day. Following one of these nightly prayer sessions, I came down off the mountain and chose My disciples, people who I would train—men who would one day build and lead My church.

Would that you, too, before any great work, would spend time with Father God in prayer. To seek His will, His wisdom, His way. To secure His blessings, His bounty, His supply. To silence any doubts, misgivings, and fears. To build up your creativity, strength, grit, perseverance, and determination. Yes, spend much time with God—He

who never fails to supply what you need. Make it a dedicated quiet time. Carve out that special space for you and Him alone, where you can abide uninterrupted. Yes, before any and every good deed, go deep. Because that's where you will find God. That's where you will gain peace and courage.

♥ ♥ ♥ ♥ ♥ ♥ ♥ ♥ ♥

One day soon afterward Jesus went up on a mountain to pray, and he prayed to God all night. At daybreak he called together all of his disciples and chose twelve of them to be apostles.

LUKE 6:12–13 NLT

Heart Test

♥ ♥ ♥ ♥ ♥ ♥ ♥ ♥ ♥

I have chosen you—and for a very good reason. You are a woman after My own heart. Yes, you have flaws. All humans do. But it is because of those flaws that I can use you. It is because you have made mistakes that you are more able to help others. It is because you have lost ones dear to you that you can do the work I have chosen you to perform.

You see, you have suffered all these things so I could know what was at the bottom of your heart, so I might know everything about you, so I could know how prepared you are to take on more of My will. In all these things you have experienced, I have been with you. And the adventures are just beginning. So do not delay for this next effort I am asking you to undertake. Spend time in prayer

with Me and you will discover our next step together. Be strong and courageous. Have confidence that I have equipped you to do all that I am calling you to do. Continually apply your learned wisdom when needed and inquire of Me when there is any doubt as to direction, timing, or mission.

♥♥♥♥♥♥♥♥♥

Hezekiah succeeded in everything he did.
But when the rulers of Babylon sent emissaries to
find out about the sign from God that had taken
place earlier, God left him on his own to see what
he would do; he wanted to test his heart.

2 CHRONICLES 32:31 MSG

Timing

♥ ♥ ♥ ♥ ♥ ♥ ♥ ♥ ♥

It's all in the timing. Father God has everything all planned out. He knew what humankind would be in the beginning. And He knew He needed Me to come in at the end. To save a people who could not save themselves. To bring light into the world, free the captives, and give sight to the blind and a voice to the mute. To die on the cross for sisters such as you. And now God has a plan for you. You are here, in this place, in this exact time, among this exact populace for a reason. There are no mistakes. You have a definite role to play. See, look around you. Contemplate what you have already experienced. Reflect on how that has built you into the woman, mother, sister, wife, daughter, friend you are today. Meditate on how you have come to the kingdom—God's

kingdom—for such a time as this. Seek from Me direction, a path, an avenue in which you can express God through yourself. For that is what you are—an expression of the Creator. Allow Him to move you, mold you. Be pliable in His hands. Go where He has called you to go. Do not hesitate.

♥ ♥ ♥ ♥ ♥ ♥ ♥ ♥ ♥

"For if you remain completely silent at this time, relief and deliverance will arise. . .from another place, but you and your father's house will perish. Yet who knows whether you have come to the kingdom for such a time as this?"

ESTHER 4:14 NKJV

Determined Follower

♥♥♥♥♥♥♥♥♥♥

Are you determined to follow Me—no matter what? Are you resolute about never leaving Me, going where I go, staying where I stay? Are all My people also your people? If you are so resolved, great things await you. For My followers must be determined to never let Me go. To continue to love Me, more and more. To know Me better than they know themselves. To be so wrapped up in Me that they lose themselves in My love, light, and longing for the kingdom of heaven. Allow no sin, no misgivings, no doubts to come between us. Be willing to forsake all others in order to stay close by My side.

With Me, you will find God's Promised Land, a sweet home for all weary yet dedicated followers. Between us is a bond no other man or

woman can break. Pledge your life to Mine and eternity is yours.

♥♥♥♥♥♥♥♥♥♥

"Entreat me not to leave you, or to turn back from following after you; for wherever you go, I will go; and wherever you lodge, I will lodge; your people shall be my people, and your God, my God. Where you die, I will die, and there will I be buried. The LORD do so to me, and more also, if anything but death parts you and me."

RUTH 1:16–17 NKJV

Be the Love

♥♥♥♥♥♥♥♥♥♥

You may be the best speaker, counselor, debater in the world. But if you do not have the love of God in you, you are nothing but a noisemaker, a talking head. If you have the gift of discernment and understand all the mysteries of this world but do not have love, you are useless, no good to anyone. If you give everything you have to those in need and sacrifice yourself on behalf of the poor but have not love, you gain nothing.

I am that love. I am the love that endures forever, is not envious, conceited, rude. I am never seeking My own good—but whatever is good for you alone.

Be the love. Be the mother who not only disciplines her child but hugs and forgives. Be the sister who never holds a grudge but looks to help her siblings in any and every way. Be the wife who does

not go to bed angry at her spouse but seeks to find common ground before the lights go out. Be the daughter who does not get exasperated with her parents but cares for them as she cares for herself. Be the church volunteer who is willing to serve wherever needed. Be the neighbor who reaches out a hand to those less fortunate than herself. Be the love this world so desperately needs. Be Me.

♥ ♥ ♥ ♥ ♥ ♥ ♥ ♥ ♥

Though I have the gift of prophecy,
and understand all mysteries and all knowledge,
and though I have all faith, so that I could remove
mountains, but have not love, I am nothing.

1 CORINTHIANS 13:2 NKJV

Your Refuge

♥♥♥♥♥♥♥♥♥♥

There is no peace unless you believe in Me. So rid yourself of all worries. Throw away all anguish. Instead, believe that I can conquer all. Know that in Me you are as safe as a babe in arms. Spend time in My presence to build up that trust. Take a risk, and watch Me move. Abide in Me, and nothing can reach you.

For I am the Rock that you need in this world where the footing can be unstable. I am the One who sends angels to protect you. I am the One constantly searching for the faithful on this planet. I am the One whose powers no enemy can withstand. I am working to save you from snares you can't even see. I am the One protecting you from all harm. So fret yourself no longer. Don't worry about the illnesses that are

taking others down. Forget about the imagined monsters underneath the bed. Nothing can reach you as long as you stay in My arms.

♥ ♥ ♥ ♥ ♥ ♥ ♥ ♥ ♥

You who sit down in the High God's presence,
spend the night in Shaddai's shadow,
say this: "GOD, you're my refuge.
I trust in you and I'm safe!"
PSALM 91:1 MSG

Starting Block

♥ ♥ ♥ ♥ ♥ ♥ ♥ ♥ ♥

There are so many things for you to learn, for Me to teach you. But are you listening? Are you reflecting? Are you considering what I may be revealing to you right now in your life? Reading the Word is great—but applying it to your life and reflecting upon it is even greater.

Spend some time looking within, checking out your heart, considering what I may be saying to you through life experiences. Then, once you know what is deep in your heart, consider what is coming out of it. Are you sensitive to the feelings of others? Are you treating yourself and those around you with compassion? Are you being patient, calm, enduring, and selfless? In these moments, let all pretensions fall away. Let down your guard. You are safe here with Me. Ignore all distractions. Simply focus on My light. Sense it

searching you within. Pause when it pauses. And reflect, saying, "Lord, reveal any darkness, any deviate way within me. Help me not to stray from but to stay by Your Word."

Allow Me to tenderize your heart, your starting block to all that follows in this day, this road, this life, and the next.

♥ ♥ ♥ ♥ ♥ ♥ ♥ ♥ ♥

Keep vigilant watch over your heart;
that's where life starts. Don't talk out of both sides
of your mouth; avoid careless banter, white lies,
and gossip. Keep your eyes straight ahead; ignore
all sideshow distractions. Watch your step, and
the road will stretch out smooth before you.
PROVERBS 4:23–26 MSG

In a Nutshell

♥♥♥♥♥♥♥♥♥

It's a simple plan, really. Love. That's it in a nutshell. Love, love, love. Forget about those who have harmed you in some way. All they've really done is harmed themselves and weakened their own spirit. So just walk away. Don't look back. Forgive and move on. Love everyone around you—no matter what their race, creed, color, nationality, status, finances. Love them all equally, for not one is better than another. Help those who cannot help themselves, who are defenseless. Look around for those who are in trouble, and ease their pain. Pray. Love. And pray some more. Then laugh. Jump in the rain puddle, slide in the snow, snicker at the sun. Take off your shoes and slide in your stocking feet across the floor.

Find the joy in life. It's there, around every

corner, just waiting for you. And when the day is done, consider your blessings, one by one. Drift off to sleep with praise upon your lips. Then begin again tomorrow. I'll be here, ready, willing, and able to lead you higher and higher.

♥ ♥ ♥ ♥ ♥ ♥ ♥ ♥ ♥

He's already made it plain how to live, what to do, what GOD is looking for in men and women. It's quite simple: Do what is fair and just to your neighbor, be compassionate and loyal in your love, and don't take yourself too seriously—take God seriously.

MICAH 6:8 MSG

Lord of Nevertheless

♥♥♥♥♥♥♥♥♥♥

I am the Lord of Nevertheless. Throughout life, women come up against a myriad of obstacles. These hindrances may come in the guise of unbelievers, discouragers, naysayers, and the like. But pay them no mind. For no matter what they say or do to thwart your efforts or the attaining of your desires, I am standing ready with a *nevertheless*, which will see you on to victory. So don't worry about the comments or actions of others. I am with you—and with Me on your side, nothing need stand in your way. But you need to believe. You need to trust Me to help you conquer all things. I am the key to your triumphs. Not in your own power, but in Mine, will you succeed at everything you set your mind to. My Word is proof, for it is there that you will read about man

and woman's myriad challenges that were over-come by My *but* or *nevertheless.*

❤ ❤ ❤ ❤ ❤ ❤ ❤ ❤ ❤

The inhabitants of the land. . .spoke to David, saying, "You shall not come in here; but the blind and the lame will repel you," thinking, "David cannot come in here." Nevertheless David took the stronghold of Zion (that is, the City of David). . . . So David went on and became great, and the LORD God of hosts was with him.

2 SAMUEL 5:6–7, 10 NKJV

Heart Thoughts

You may be able to fool others, but you cannot fool Me. I know the truth of the matter. I know what really lies within your heart. I know what you are thinking. Do you? Are you watching the thoughts that are going through your own mind, the ones you are claiming as reality? Take a look now. Are you thinking the chances are you will catch the cold that's going around? If so, you will. For what you think deep within ultimately becomes your reality.

Change those heart thoughts and you will change your life. Be vigilant. Keep a searchlight within. If you are full of misgivings, your confidence is sure to wane. If you are full of doubt, your faith will falter. If you are full of hate, darkness will pervade. If you cannot pardon the

actions or words of another, you will be ingesting the bitter poison of unforgiveness. Your heart often does not reflect the true reality of this God life you are attempting to live. So stop. Check the thoughts in your heart. Compare them to My Word. Then take whatever actions are necessary to align them to My truth—and My truth alone: victory, love, compassion, joy, praise, selflessness, and so on. This is the true heart, the heart of My Spirit linked with your own.

♥ ♥ ♥ ♥ ♥ ♥ ♥ ♥ ♥

For as he thinks in his heart, so is he.
PROVERBS 23:7 AMP

God's Device

♥♥♥♥♥♥♥♥♥

There are some things in this life that you cannot change. One of them is that humans die. And once they have passed from this world to the next, things will never be the same again—for those who have passed and for the ones they leave behind. But do not despair! Something better awaits believers who go to the other side.

And those who are still alive and are apart from God, those who have exiled themselves from His presence, still may find their way back. God's arm is stretched out, reaching to them, seeking to bring them closer and closer to Him. Meanwhile, He is patiently waiting for them to make a move toward Him. In the meantime, God is working through you to love the outcasts—no matter what they have done. To have compassion

for them—no matter whom they have hurt. Allow the Father's light to shine through you, to illumine the corners of darkness, to draw others to Me—the Son who can, and has, changed the world forever and ever, amen. Be God's device, and bring in the light.

♥ ♥ ♥ ♥ ♥ ♥ ♥ ♥ ♥

We must all die; we are like water spilled on the ground, which cannot be gathered up again. And God does not take away life, but devises means so that he who is banished may not be an utter outcast from Him.

2 SAMUEL 14:14 AMP

Vitally Knowing God

♥ ♥ ♥ ♥ ♥ ♥ ♥ ♥ ♥ ♥

Knowledge is a great thing. But even greater is an intimate understanding of the One who rules the universe—the God of your life. You will find Him, you will understand Him, you will "get" Him when you find, understand, and "get" Me. For I was God in the flesh.

You will recognize the Master, the Father, by fully understanding Me, His Son. My descriptors are numerous and all point back to Abba God. I am love, light, manna from heaven; a man of sorrows, a worker of miracles; Living Water to the thirsty; healer of lepers, lame, dumb, mute, deaf, possessed. I have walked the depths of the abyss and ascended the stairways to heaven. I calmed the seas and tamed the wind. I sacrificed My very life to save yours. Seek Me as you seek nothing

else, as a vital part of your existence. Know Me
and you will understand all that My Father is, all
that I am, all that the Holy Spirit provides, and
all that you can be!

♥♥♥♥♥♥♥♥♥

*Know the God of your father [have personal
knowledge of Him, be acquainted with,
and understand Him; appreciate, heed,
and cherish Him] and serve Him with a
blameless heart and a willing mind. For the
Lord searches all hearts and minds and
understands all the wanderings of the thoughts.
If you seek Him [inquiring for and of Him
and requiring Him as your first and vital
necessity] you will find Him.*

1 CHRONICLES 28:9 AMP

All You Need

❤ ❤ ❤ ❤ ❤ ❤ ❤ ❤ ❤

At this very moment, I am standing before God for you. It is love that has brought Me to this place. And it is love that makes Me stay. There is nothing I will not do for you. I laid down My life for you and would gladly do so over and over again if it would bring you closer and closer to God. But I could only do it once—and once was enough.

Now I am the bridge that stands between you and your Creator. Nothing can ever take you away from the all-powerful Master of the universe. And no one would ever dare mess with one of His own. So do not fear. Nothing and no one can separate you from God's love—not hunger, poverty, discouragement, threats, terror, heart-

ache, violence. You are His and His alone for all time. That is why I came. That is why I am still here, fighting for you every step of the way. Loving you every minute of the day. Run to Us when you need help. Stay with Us when you need comfort. Move with Us when it is time for action. Rest in Us when you need strength. We are all you need. And We are always here, waiting, even when you sleep.

♥ ♥ ♥ ♥ ♥ ♥ ♥ ♥ ♥

Who then will condemn us? No one—for Christ
Jesus died for us and was raised to life for us,
and he is sitting in the place of honor at
God's right hand, pleading for us.
ROMANS 8:34 NLT

Craving the Word

♥♥♥♥♥♥♥♥♥♥

There is something about God's Word that changes lives, frees souls, lifts spirits, and conquers worlds. It is more powerful than any other force. It delves into hearts and rewrites history.

Come seek the knowledge of the Word—of Me. Prepare your heart to understand the truth of God. Don't just read it—crave it. See it as a vital necessity. Ask questions. Pray that the Word would lead you to become the person your Maker designed you to be. Do not miss out on this opportunity to rewire yourself so that you function fully from the spiritual and physical aspects already implanted in you. There can be no greater goal in life, for those who crave the Word with all their heart, soul, strength, and spirit are mighty movers and shakers for God.

The scriptures are what made Me the greatest miracle worker the world has ever seen. Imagine what they can do for you—and what you can do for God!

♥♥♥♥♥♥♥♥♥

Upon him was the good hand of his God.
For Ezra had prepared and set his heart to seek
the Law of the Lord [to inquire for it and of it,
to require and yearn for it], and to do and teach
in Israel its statutes and its ordinances.

EZRA 7:9–10 AMP

291

A God-Empowered Life

♥♥♥♥♥♥♥♥♥

It is not mere words that move the hearts of women. It is the power of God behind them. It is the power of a life committed to the Master of the universe. Who or what is empowering your life? Who or what has the most influence over you? Instead of striving to be the best at some role, why not strive to be the best God follower? Let go of the role-playing as a mother, wife, sister, daughter, friend, teacher, or girlfriend. Put all those things behind you—and put God before you in all things. Allow Me to give you the strength required to be a woman of the Way. I have plenty for each and every situation you will encounter, for each person you will ever meet. Allow Me to fuel all your endeavors so that when people see you, all they see is My love.

You are more than any role you could ever play. You are a daughter of God. You hold a royal position in His kingdom. Take hold of the scepter of His love. Stop the talk and the playing. Begin living the Word, feeling its power, and changing the world, one person at a time.

♥ ♥ ♥ ♥ ♥ ♥ ♥ ♥ ♥

*God's Way is not a matter of mere talk;
it's an empowered life.*
1 CORINTHIANS 4:20 MSG

Fear Nothing

❤ ❤ ❤ ❤ ❤ ❤ ❤ ❤ ❤

You are a woman of strength, honor, determination, and integrity. All the difficulties you have been through have made you so. Yet at the same time, you are soft, gentle, kind, and loving. That is from all the compassion you have received and felt along the way, whether from Me or one of My followers. You are a chosen one. God has been hovering over this world, from one end to the other, and has found you. He has stretched out His arms to pick you up, to cling to you, to bring you to Him, to His side. It is there that you have found Me. Abiding in Me, you have nothing to fear. No evil can reach you.

So do not fret over terrors told of by men. Do not let the devil's shadows darken your door. He is nothing but a puff of smoke. Turn your eyes

away from him and onto Me. Fear nothing. I have all the strength, courage, and comfort you will ever need. I will never let go of you but will continue to give you victory each and every step of the way. Be who you are.

♥♥♥♥♥♥♥♥♥

Fear not [there is nothing to fear], for I am with you; do not look around you in terror and be dismayed, for I am your God. I will strengthen and harden you to difficulties, yes, I will help you; yes, I will hold you up and retain you with My [victorious] right hand of rightness and justice.

ISAIAH 41:10 AMP

A Better Way

♥♥♥♥♥♥♥♥♥♥

Sometimes things don't work out like you had hoped or planned. Take heart, woman. God has a better plan. It may not seem so right now. In fact, things may look pretty hopeless. But God always has a better way. And someday you will understand. In the meantime, remember how much He cares for you. He gave you Me, to love and to cherish. To keep you from now into eternity. I am here to give you hope, to remind you that things that may look pretty bleak are actually the beginning of something great and grand. So continue to keep your chin up. Do not let discouragement have its way. Forget about what has happened and move forward, knowing that something bigger and better awaits. Have patience as you keep on keeping on. Keep your eyes on the prize—Me,

God, the Word, the Spirit, eternal life. And God will take care of the rest.

♥♥♥♥♥♥♥♥♥

May our Lord Jesus Christ himself and God our Father, who loved us and by his grace gave us eternal encouragement and good hope, encourage your hearts and strengthen you in every good deed and word.

2 Thessalonians 2:16–17 NIV

Joyful in Jesus

❤❤❤❤❤❤❤❤❤❤

One of the true tests of the spiritual nature is when things don't go your way. It's easy to be happy and joyful when your stomach and closet are both full—when the kids are doing well in school, the boss is more than happy with your work, your husband is treating you like a queen, your mom is in good health, your sister is full of helpful advice, and your friend is finding nothing but encouraging things to say to and about you. But what happens when your son starts spending more time in detention than in an advanced-placement class, the boss does nothing but complain about your work, your husband is tired of the same old casserole, your mom needs special care, your sister points out what you're doing "wrong," and your friend is gossiping behind your back?

Either way, through good times and bad, a true woman of the Way finds a reason to praise God and be joyful in Jesus. What can you praise and smile about today?

♥♥♥♥♥♥♥♥♥

Though the fig tree does not bud and there are no grapes on the vines, though the olive crop fails and the fields produce no food, though there are no sheep in the pen and no cattle in the stalls, yet I will rejoice in the LORD, I will be joyful in God my Savior.

HABAKKUK 3:17–18 NIV

Superhuman Power

The Word of God—what a powerhouse of information. From this Word you can fuel your life and love the unlovable. With this Word you can move mountains and do more than I ever attempted to do when I was walking the earth. Under this Word you can find protection from evil. Behind this Word you can rest in the shadows of truth. Over this Word you can fly, meet up with Me in the heavens, and draw closer to God on His throne. In this Word you can trust, and by this Word you may live an abundant life. Whether written, spoken, or read, this Word contains the power to help you do all you have been called to do. It is working out a life like no other, one only you can live. Trust it. Exercise it. Stick to it. And depend upon it to serve you like nothing and no one else can.

♥ ♥ ♥ ♥ ♥ ♥ ♥ ♥ ♥ ♥

And we also [especially] thank God continually for this, that when you received the message of God [which you heard] from us, you welcomed it not as the word of [mere] men, but as it truly is, the Word of God, which is effectually at work in you who believe [exercising its superhuman power in those who adhere to and trust in and rely on it].

1 Thessalonians 2:13 AMP

A Woman Warrior

❤❤❤❤❤❤❤❤❤

It has been said that women are the weaker sex. Yet they were the ones who supported Me during My earthly ministry. They are the ones who stayed by My side when I was on the cross. They were also the first to appear at the tomb, see Me alive, and recognize Me. When these women saw Me, they saw love personified. And their attraction to love remained with Me until the end—and at the beginning.

You may be considered weak, but you are in so many ways strong. After all, you continue to birth babies, nurture the pained, endure the monthly "curse," serve without being asked, pray for others, and more, so much more. You need not bandy about your strength, showing off in front of the other sex. But you can have a quiet knowing, a

feeling that you have depths to you that man will never know or realize. You are a woman warrior of the Way. Continue in the same vein as the sisters who have gone before—unafraid, enamored by true love, and willing to do what you have been called to do, to go wherever you have been prompted to go—and more!

♥♥♥♥♥♥♥♥♥

Beat your plowshares into swords, and your pruning hooks into spears; let the weak say, I am strong [a warrior]!
JOEL 3:10 AMP

Blasts of Dynamic Power

♥♥♥♥♥♥♥♥♥

Prayer is the channel through which God's power streams down to you and bursts into your life, changing the cast, the scenery, the events of your day, changing you, your life, your soul, your heart, and those around you. When you let Me into every detail of your life via prayer, I move in and on every aspect, molding, shaping, empowering. The force, strength, and energy of My living water carves deep valleys and channels in the landscape of your life. My rivulets don't just meander—they have a purpose, as do you and your life. So call on this mighty force.

Use prayer, your conduit, channel, lifeline to Me. Call upon Me for every little detail. Make Me a part of your constant conversation. With eyes open wide or shut tight, say My name:

"Jesus." And before you know it, I will be carving out a road on which you can walk. Or lifting you high above the fray so that you will not stumble. Or simply surrounding you with a hedge of protection so that no one and nothing can harm you, My beloved.

♥ ♥ ♥ ♥ ♥ ♥ ♥ ♥ ♥ ♥

Pray [also] for one another, that you may be healed and restored [to a spiritual tone of mind and heart]. The earnest (heartfelt, continued) prayer of a righteous man makes tremendous power available [dynamic in its working].

JAMES 5:16 AMP

From Trial to Triumph

♥♥♥♥♥♥♥♥♥

When I walked among you, I spent much time alone with Father God, gleaning His wisdom, basking in His presence, allowing His precious Spirit to fill Me, lead Me, direct Me. His Word was My soul food, preparing Me for the onslaught to come. I turned away from the world in order to fully focus on the one and only true Lord.

God alone gave Me the power to fend off the arrows of temptation in My wilderness trial with the devil. God's Word protected Me from every dart thrown by the dark one. You, too, have the power to defend yourself from the evil one's schemes: My Word. Learn it. Know it. Understand it. Make it a part of your very being. Begin by finding a passage that not only speaks to your heart but also gives you a sense, a hint of the

power of God. Words that can lift you up when you fall into the pit of despair. Words that can shield you from a world overrun with negativity, shadows, and terrors. In so doing, you will enter all trials prepared and will come out of the wilderness as did I—in triumph. And that good word will spread.

♥♥♥♥♥♥♥♥♥

Now Jesus, full of the Holy Spirit, left the Jordan and was led by the Spirit into the wild. . . .
Jesus returned to Galilee powerful in the Spirit.
News that he was back spread
through the countryside.

LUKE 4:1, 14 MSG

Back to Basics

♥♥♥♥♥♥♥♥♥

Feeling confused, overwhelmed, directionless? It's time to wipe all slates clean. Start over. Get back to the basics. Take everything else off your schedule, and rest in Me. Simply love Me with every fiber of your being. Give Me some good one-on-one time, the kind of quality time you spend with a lover, friend, husband, or infant. Find a quiet corner. Eliminate all distractions. Light a candle. Breathe deep. And allow your spirit to seek out Mine.

I am always here, waiting for you to stop your rushing around, heedless of Me and My presence until a crisis situation presents itself. Then you are driven to your knees, sobbing, clutching, grasping in desperation. Don't let it get to that point! Seek Me first in your own mind, spirit, heart, and soul.

Allow Me to fill you with strength, peace, power, and joy. Then throughout your day, remember Me. See Me working right beside you. When you do, you will experience My hand ordering your world, changing the landscape for your benefit and My glory.

♥ ♥ ♥ ♥ ♥ ♥ ♥ ♥ ♥

And you shall love the Lord your God with all your [mind and] heart and with your entire being and with all your might. And these words which I am commanding you this day shall be [first] in your [own] minds and hearts.

DEUTERONOMY 6:5–6 AMP

Surging Energy

♥♥♥♥♥♥♥♥♥

Come to Me for all your needs—physical, spiritual, mental, emotional. Whatever ails you, I have the cure. When you reach out to Me, My energy begins to surge. It cannot help but respond to your each and every request, to pour out and touch your life. So leave everything else behind. Drop whatever you are doing. And come to Me. Seek My face above all else. Reach out, extend yourself, and I will automatically react in the only way I know how—through pure love. It is the great, grand master of all things. It is God. He is the light that will chase away your gloom.

So come to Me. Partake of His power. There is a never-ending portion of potency for all who believe. But to receive you must come. Let go of your doubts. Empty your hands of disbelief.

Open your heart to all that I am. And I will fill you to the brim, saving you from the world and your very self. I will cut away any chains that bind you. Sister, come to Me and drink well from Me, your source, your Savior, your King.

♥ ♥ ♥ ♥ ♥ ♥ ♥ ♥ ♥

And all the multitude were seeking to touch Him, for healing power was all the while going forth from Him and curing them all [saving them from severe illnesses or calamities].

LUKE 6:19 AMP

311

Around Every Corner

♥♥♥♥♥♥♥♥♥♥

There is one sure way to destroy a relationship with anyone—through neglect. When you no longer pay attention to a child, she will soon become hungry, naked, miserable, and homeless. Ignore a lover and he will soon become restless, resentful, and a rover. The same thing happened thousands of years ago. God's temple was destroyed because the kings of Judah had neglected it. In fact, the people had even lost sight of the Book of the Law that God had given Moses! Sister, this should not be! Do not neglect your time with Me! Do not allow our relationship to fall to dust. Instead, build up our rapport. Spend time in My Word. Look for Me around every corner—of heaven and earth, of hopes and dreams, of home and work. I am always with you! Let there be

no doubt in your heart or mind! Come into My presence and I will remain in yours. Bring Me your sacrifice of praise—and you will find even more things to thank Me for.

♥♥♥♥♥♥♥♥♥

They delivered it to the workmen who had oversight of the Lord's house, who gave it to repair and restore the temple: to the carpenters and builders to buy hewn stone, and timber for couplings and beams for the houses which the kings of Judah had destroyed [by neglect].

2 CHRONICLES 34:10–11 AMP

A Good Woman

♥♥♥♥♥♥♥♥♥♥

How can you tell what's in your heart? By what comes out of your mouth. What have you been saying lately? Are your words encouraging or critical? Are you a woman who sucks the energy out of a room as soon as you enter it—or are you a woman who tends to give off good vibrations wherever you go? Whichever you are, know this: the words you say will show people what is truly in your heart. If you are an honorable and good woman, people will want to be around you, for you lift them up. You make them feel important, that they matter, because you listen with love in your heart. But if you are leaning away from the light, people will want to avoid you, cast their eyes down, and hope to leave unnoticed because they instinctively know that the words you direct

their way are likely to be painful to them. The funny thing is, painful words harm not only the receiver but the speaker and other listeners as well. So take a good look at what is coming out of your mouth, for that will be sure to reveal what is truly in your heart.

♥ ♥ ♥ ♥ ♥ ♥ ♥ ♥ ♥

"A good person produces good things from the treasury of a good heart, and an evil person produces evil things from the treasury of an evil heart. What you say flows from what is in your heart."

LUKE 6:45 NLT

Storm Whisperer

♥♥♥♥♥♥♥♥♥

Sometimes life feels like a roller coaster ride. First you are up in the air, laughing with exhilaration. The view from the top is tremendous. But then before you know it, you are whooshing back down, heading for the earth at an amazing speed. Your stomach jumps up to your heart, and you fear you may soon crash and burn. In the midst of it all, where is your focus? On the white knuckles that are gripping the safety bar as you hang on for dear life? Or are you fixated on the black macadam that seems only too eager to greet you face-first?

In the perfect roller coaster rides or ocean storms of life, look to and cry out to Me. I am the One who can save you. Remember Me in your trouble! I will bring you out safely to the other

side. I alone can calm the wind and the waves. I alone can give you smooth sailing. With Me in your life, you are no longer riding alone. Simply acknowledge Me and you will feel My presence by your side. With Me at the helm of your life, you will safely reach your destination.

♥ ♥ ♥ ♥ ♥ ♥ ♥ ♥ ♥ ♥

Then they cry to the Lord in their trouble,
and He brings them out of their distresses.
He hushes the storm to a calm and to a gentle
whisper, so that the waves of the sea are still.
Then the men are glad because of the calm,
and He brings them to their desired haven.

PSALM 107:28–30 AMP

God: The Promise Maker— and Keeper

♥♥♥♥♥♥♥♥♥♥

Promises, promises, promises. You've heard them over and over from the people in your life. In fact, chances are you have made a few promises yourself. But have you and others kept them? When your child says, "I'll do my homework," you'd like to believe her. But the next time you walk into her room, she's playing with her dolls. Your husband vows to get to the honey-do list this weekend. But you've heard that line a thousand times before and the sink still leaks and the garbage disposal remains on the fritz.

In the midst of all these broken, unkept, but well-intended vows is One who stands alone: God. He will never break His promises to you. That's because God cannot lie. What He says is the truth. He promises to love you, to treat you

like the apple of His eye. He promises never to leave you or forsake you. He promises to respond when you call Him, to give you the desires of your heart, to reserve a place for you in heaven. And He promises that I, His Son, will save you from all that enslaves you. In fact, in Me, you are already free. So come. Take God up on His promises. Hitch your wagon to Me, and together we will ride to the stars. I promise.

♥♥♥♥♥♥♥♥♥

*The LORD has taken an oath
and will not break his vow.*
PSALM 110:4 NLT

319

Let Peace Reign

Woman, do not allow confusion to reign in your life. Stop all the multitasking. Go ahead and make the list if you must. But don't try to do more than you have actual energy for. And do not try to do more than one thing at a time. A woman of the Way is not to run helter-skelter but to walk with a calm assurance that what needs to get done in one day will, in fact, be done. And once that day is done, she is to rest in calm assurance that God is with her and will provide her with what she needs tomorrow. In fact, He's already making plans for her welfare.

So stop focusing on what you didn't get done. Instead, focus on God's order of priorities: First and foremost, seek God. Then take care of yourself. Next comes your husband (if you have one),

your kids (if you have any), and church. Then and only then is a career to be considered. If you are feeling chaotic, take a look at who is holding the reins in your life: is it the orderly God of peace or the disordered devil of chaos?

♥ ♥ ♥ ♥ ♥ ♥ ♥ ♥ ♥ ♥

For God is not a God of disorder but of peace.
1 CORINTHIANS 14:33 NIV

Be the Christ

♥♥♥♥♥♥♥♥♥♥

One of the best ways to share what you know about Me and God is to live your faith. To be the Word. Be the light, the understanding, the love, the selfless giver. Be the forgiveness, the joy, the treasure in a clay jar. Be the good Samaritan, the widow with the mite, the prophet Anna in the temple. Be the woman of the Way who knows that nothing with her Lord is impossible. Be the mother who lovingly gentles a child, the wife who never goes to bed angry, the sister who shows up when the going gets tough, the worker who takes her responsibilities seriously, the neighbor who shows up on a doorstep with hot chicken soup. Be the lover of Christ who knows it's better to give than receive, to cherish the unlovable, to free the oppressed. Be the

woman who does not judge, murmur, complain, or criticize. Be Christ to your family, friends, coworkers, and strangers. Spread to others all the good things you have found in Me. And watch the world change, one person at a time.

♥ ♥ ♥ ♥ ♥ ♥ ♥ ♥ ♥

And I am praying that you will put into action the generosity that comes from your faith as you understand and experience all the good things we have in Christ.

PHILEMON 1:6 NLT

God's Plan in Hand

♥ ♥ ♥ ♥ ♥ ♥ ♥ ♥ ♥

God has a plan for your life. A plan that, if you are willing, He would like to work through you. So be patient, sister. Do not be quick to take matters into your own hands. Simply continue to abide in Me. Let Me finish the good work in you that God began.

If a door of opportunity has been closed, do not fret. Do not panic. Do not abandon your path. Simply continue to praise Me in the foyer. Thank Me for the blessings you have had in the past, the ones you are enjoying in the present, and the ones that are surely streaming your way. If you feel as if you are in limbo, relax. Other things are being put into place. Don't run ahead of Me. As soon as you feel your peace has been disrupted, stop. Reflect. Consider. Seek Me and My face. Ask for

My guidance. If necessary, wait. In good time, I will give you direction so you can move safely ahead. The possibilities for your life and work are endless. Trust Me to pave the best road for you to take. Trust Me to lead you in the right direction. Trust Me to not only save you but provide you with an abundant life.

♥♥♥♥♥♥♥♥♥♥

You reach out your hand, and the power of your right hand saves me. The LORD will work out his plans for my life—for your faithful love, O LORD, endures forever. Don't abandon me, for you made me.

PSALM 138:7–8 NLT

Truly Blessed

♥♥♥♥♥♥♥♥♥♥

Look all around you. Notice the trees in bloom, the wildflowers by the road, the crescent moon hovering in the dark sky above. Inhale the sweet fragrance of spring as you watch the clouds lazily drift in the blue heavens. Listen for the call of birds, the chatter of squirrels, the hum of bees, the snicker of a well-fed horse. Witness the cud-chewing cow cooling her heels in a creek, the quick-moving shadow of a hawk, the brain-jarring pecking of a free-range chicken. All these things represent the love God has for you—and for all those who have gone before and all those who are to come. It is the cycle of life that has continued for umpteen generations—and will continue until the day I return. In the meantime, do not take your Lord and Savior for granted.

Worship the One who provides you with more than enough, the One whose hand has been upon you since the day you were conceived. Praise our Father for all He has done for you, a daughter of the King. Look for His everlasting goodness in all things. You are truly blessed.

♥♥♥♥♥♥♥♥♥

For the LORD is good and his love endures forever; his faithfulness continues through all generations.

PSALM 100:5 NIV

Closing the Gap

♥ ♥ ♥ ♥ ♥ ♥ ♥ ♥ ♥

As I look out upon the world, I see so many people who are suffering for lack of food, water, clothing, shelter, and other necessities of life. I feel their pain and their neediness. I also see people who have more than enough, people who are rich in all that others lack. And I wonder why they sit on their hands, why they do not ease the pain of their fellow man and woman.

Sister, in this world, in this moment, on this current stage, you must be able to share some of your blessings with those less fortunate. You must have an opportunity to be My hands and fill the need of another soul, whether it be donating a dress in your closet, a pair of shoes almost brand new, food from your pantry, furniture from your attic, anything that will help one who is helpless.

You must have an opportunity to share your time by volunteering to build a house, babysitting a child, driving someone to the doctor, walking for a cancer victim. You who have been given so much are My representative to those who lack. Where will you stand to help close the gap for Me today?

♥ ♥ ♥ ♥ ♥ ♥ ♥ ♥ ♥

And do not forget to do good and to share with others, for with such sacrifices God is pleased.
HEBREWS 13:16 NIV

Sole Desire

❤❤❤❤❤❤❤❤❤

I would gladly die on the cross all over again so that I could save you from a life that was imbued with darkness, one that was all about how to satisfy your own desires and nothing more. You have been changed. Your spirit calls out to Mine. And it was all done just because our Father God loved you—before you even thought of Him. You have been on His mind from the beginning of time. He wants to walk with you in the garden. His sole desire is for you to want Him as much as He wants you.

When you make your main business getting to know God and Me better, when you begin to understand it's all about His love and mercy and nothing that you could ever do, everything else in your world will adjust itself. Come. Spend time with Us. Love us as We have loved you.

♥ ♥ ♥ ♥ ♥ ♥ ♥ ♥ ♥ ♥

It wasn't so long ago that we ourselves were stupid and stubborn, dupes of sin, ordered every which way by our glands, going around with a chip on our shoulder, hated and hating back. But when God, our kind and loving Savior God, stepped in, he saved us from all that. It was all his doing; we had nothing to do with it. He gave us a good bath, and we came out of it new people, washed inside and out by the Holy Spirit.

TITUS 3:3-5 MSG

Seasons of Life

♥ ♥ ♥ ♥ ♥ ♥ ♥ ♥ ♥

Everything happens in God's timing. It is He who planned the earth's seasons of spring, summer, fall, and winter. Amazingly enough, a woman's body also has its own seasons. In the spring of life, you are enjoying your youth, when everything is fresh and new. Then comes the summer. You are now officially a woman, with a body that is ready to bear children. Then comes the fall, as your body begins to change yet once again and becomes a weather system in itself. And finally the winter of life arrives where your hair turns permanently gray and you are about to enjoy the golden years of life. In each of these stages, remember that no matter what is happening, no matter what you look like, I still love you. From puberty to perimenopause, you mean the world to Me. There is never a time when you are of more or less value to Me—you are always the most precious treasure with a pressing purpose. So just continue to go with the flow of My power. Love and see yourself as I love and see you—in every season of life.

♥♥♥♥♥♥♥♥♥

*There's an opportune time to do things,
a right time for everything on the earth: A right
time for birth and another for death, a right
time to plant and another to reap, a right time to kill
and another to heal, a right time to destroy and
another to construct, a right time to cry
and another to laugh.*

ECCLESIASTES 3:1–4 MSG

In God We Trust

♥♥♥♥♥♥♥♥♥

Ah, how hard it is for a rich woman to enter the kingdom of God. She is so busy holding on to her money and earning even more of it that she cannot let go of it and enjoy God's true riches—helping others, experiencing a magnificent sunset, enjoying the love of a good man, holding a newborn in her arms, seeing a child take her first steps, watching a bride walk down the aisle. Even more wonderful than all these things is giving one's money to someone truly in need. Yes, it's good to be sensible with your money. But it is even better to let go of things you don't really need so that you can help someone else who desperately requires a helping hand.

It is so easy for money to slip through the fingers, to be here one day and gone the next, to be sucked up by some other greedy person who only wants more and more riches—and will do

anything to obtain them. Don't let that be your method of operation, the way you go through life. Forget about trusting in money—whether you have a little or a lot. In the end, it cannot save you. But I can. Trust in Me and My will for your life—and use your money as a tool to help others, not as a god to worship or a blessing to hang on to with white-knuckled fists.

♥♥♥♥♥♥♥♥♥

Teach those who are rich in this world not to be proud and not to trust in their money, which is so unreliable. Their trust should be in God, who richly gives us all we need for our enjoyment. Tell them to use their money to do good.

1 TIMOTHY 6:17–18 NLT

A Blessed Viewpoint

❤ ❤ ❤ ❤ ❤ ❤ ❤ ❤ ❤

Earthly death holds much sorrow for a non-believer because she sees it as the true end of existence. But a woman of the Way knows she will see her loved one again someday. A nonbeliever thinks heaven is a hoax. A woman of the Way knows there is a place reserved there for her. A nonbeliever sees amassing earthly riches as the only way to get ahead in this world. A woman of the Way knows she can't take it with her and others need it more. A nonbeliever scoffs at those who praise God, whom she views as an opiate for the masses. A woman of the Way knows that God is a definite Person and views everything through His Word. A nonbeliever has a hollow joy, a haunted look, an earthly nature. A woman of the Way has the true joy of Christ,

a supernatural glow, and a heavenly nature, for her Savior has taken the sting out of life—and death! Everything looks different through a believer's eyes because she trusts in God no matter what is happening in her life. What do you see?

♥ ♥ ♥ ♥ ♥ ♥ ♥ ♥ ♥ ♥

*"But blessed is the man who trusts me, G*OD*, the woman who sticks with G*OD*. They're like trees replanted in Eden, putting down roots near the rivers—never a worry through the hottest of summers, never dropping a leaf, serene and calm through droughts, bearing fresh fruit every season."*

JEREMIAH 17:7–8 MSG

Vital Link

❤❤❤❤❤❤❤❤❤

Prayer—what a valuable tool. It's so valuable that I taught you how to do it! Prayer is your vital link to Me, for I bring it all before God on your behalf. So do not be shy. Seek Me out in each and every situation. Come before Me with all your troubles— big and small. Nothing is too little to escape My notice, to receive My care and concern.

If you have strayed, run right back into My arms. I am holding them open just for you. Turn back to Me, here and now. Ask Me any question. Give Me every request. Open the door of your heart, spirit, mind, and soul. Let's have an intimate conversation. Then you will begin to see things through My eyes. Even if your prayer is only a sigh because you cannot find the words, I will respond. Breathe Me into every space, every

corner, every area of your life. Just call out, "Jesus, Jesus, Jesus!" and I will come running. For I am only a sigh, a breath, a simple prayer away.

♥ ♥ ♥ ♥ ♥ ♥ ♥ ♥ ♥

Seek, inquire for, and require the Lord while He may be found [claiming Him by necessity and by right]; call upon Him while He is near.
ISAIAH 55:6 AMP

Quietness and Confidence

♥♥♥♥♥♥♥♥♥

You have been blessed with the Holy Spirit to help you in your journey and with Me to give you guidance as you abide in Me. Simply imbibe My living water, read My Word, and live your life accordingly. With all these "helps," you know what's right and what's wrong. God's law—to love Him, yourself, and others—is already written on your heart. The result of living as a woman of the Way, living a life of love, is a supernatural quietness and confidence.

A Christ follower knows she need not fret over anything—big or little. She knows where to go for direction and strength—straight to the Word. She knows that although many people are harried, she doesn't have to be. Why bother when you are going to live forever? Keep that mind-set

and you will be assured of reaping calmness and confidence on earth and in heaven. That's a gift of love from Me to you.

♥♥♥♥♥♥♥♥♥♥

You women who are so complacent, rise up and listen to me; you daughters who feel secure, hear what I have to say! . . . The LORD's justice will dwell in the desert, his righteousness live in the fertile field. The fruit of that righteousness will be peace; its effect will be quietness and confidence forever.

ISAIAH 32:9, 16–17 NIV

Eyes Lifted

❤❤❤❤❤❤❤❤❤

Look up! I am here! I am waiting for you to turn to Me for help. I, the Maker of heaven and earth, can move mountains, carve valleys, split the earth, and rule the ocean. No matter what your problem, situation, predicament, I can show you a way out—or will help you get through it. With Me on your team, there is no reason to fear. I will not allow anyone or anything to injure you. That is why I, unlike My disciples in the Garden of Gethsemane, am ever vigilant, always awake, on the job twenty-four hours a day, seven days a week. There is nothing that I do not see. There is nothing that I cannot change. I am here doing My part. You need only do yours—by looking up. Seek My face, My strength, My confidence, My provision, My peace, My miracle-working power.

I am the only help you will ever need in this life—and the next.

♥ ♥ ♥ ♥ ♥ ♥ ♥ ♥ ♥

I will lift up my eyes to the hills—from whence comes my help? My help comes from the LORD, who made heaven and earth. He will not allow your foot to be moved; He who keeps you will not slumber.

PSALM 121:1–3 NKJV

The Rescuing Knight

♥♥♥♥♥♥♥♥♥

I am the hero, the conqueror within you. I am your mother, father, brother, sister, friend—I am all things to you. With Me in your life, you are safe from all danger. You can stand on your own two feet. I am the shining knight that continually rescues you from all harm—within and without. Cry out to Me and I come running, for no foe can withstand My power. No enemy cannot be overcome.

Feel Me surrounding you, a protective shield that cannot be penetrated by the poisonous arrows of man or woman. Allow no words, actions, or thoughts to bother you. I take them all upon Myself. As soon as I hear your cry, I sweep you into My presence. Thus no storm, no fire, no flood, no calamity, no grief can truly overtake you.

♥ ♥ ♥ ♥ ♥ ♥ ♥ ♥ ♥

I love you, GOD—you make me strong.
GOD is bedrock under my feet, the castle in
which I live, my rescuing knight. My God—the
high crag where I run for dear life, hiding behind
the boulders, safe in the granite hideout.
I sing to GOD, the Praise-Lofty, and find
myself safe and saved.

PSALM 18:1–3 MSG

345

Know Me

♥♥♥♥♥♥♥♥♥

Story is a powerful tool. It helps to communicate truths that can be revealed in no other way. That is why when I was among you I spoke in parables. You can use that same storytelling tool to help others understand. To help spread the word. To reveal Me—the ultimate Truth. Read the Gospel stories to understand Me. Know Me, My story, My life, My teachings. Forget debates. Just tell My story. Then live My message—love others, yourself, and neighbors.

Be gentle, kind, trustworthy, not given to gossip. Treat older women with respect. Learn from them. Be a servant to all, and so lead them into love. Honor your husband, respect your parents, don't exasperate your children. And above all, remember that I walked among you. I was the

physical manifestation of God on earth. And if you follow in My footsteps, you, too, will be an expression, an extension of the Father. Know Me. Live Me. And others will learn to know Me—then follow. No one can resist a good story—and Mine is the best!

♥ ♥ ♥ ♥ ♥ ♥ ♥ ♥ ♥

I resolved to know nothing (to be acquainted with nothing, to make a display of the knowledge of nothing, and to be conscious of nothing) among you except Jesus Christ (the Messiah) and Him crucified.
1 CORINTHIANS 2:2 AMP

Soft Hearts

❤❤❤❤❤❤❤❤❤

I hold this day in My hands—in trust for you. Make of it what you will. Look for opportunities behind each and every door. Seek to love each life you come into contact with. Look with curiosity at what may be revealed. Be gentle with yourself and those around you. And with all joy, tackle each task before you, knowing that all you receive is from My hand. Listen for My voice, seek My path, walk My way, and you will never find yourself alone, frightened, or out of My will.

Keep your heart soft, pliable, malleable, open to My suggestion, My leading. Step in time with your spirit, allowing it free rein as it links up with Mine. There is nothing more beautiful in this world than a woman of God, quietly obeying My commands and finding contentment in

loving and serving others. Stay close, woman. I have need of you today.

♥♥♥♥♥♥♥♥♥

O come, let us worship and bow down,
let us kneel before the Lord our Maker [in
reverent praise and supplication]. For He is our
God and we are the people of His pasture and
the sheep of His hand. Today, if you will hear His
voice, harden not your hearts.

PSALM 95:6–8 AMP

Making Room

♥♥♥♥♥♥♥♥♥♥

You are so eager to know what tomorrow may bring. You are so attached to plans of your own making, for women rarely want to be surprised. But I am asking you to detach from the outcome of your life, to be okay with *not* knowing the end of the story. Instead, have faith that I am leading you in the right direction. You may have a general idea of how you'd like your life to come out, but I am the One who will take you step by step to reach the dream God has had in mind for you from the beginning.

So trust Me. Know that all I want is for your good—and the good of those whose lives you will touch. Just take My hand. Be confident that I will not lead you astray but place you exactly where you were meant to be. In fact, that's where

you are today—just where I want you to be. So relax. Live with joy in the moment, in the now. Continue to make your plans but leave room for Me to move in your journey. For only with Me will you reach places you would never dream of. For only with Me will you have the courage, the fortitude, and the perseverance to become all you were made to be.

♥ ♥ ♥ ♥ ♥ ♥ ♥ ♥ ♥ ♥

We can make our plans, but the LORD determines our steps.
PROVERBS 16:9 NLT

Son Rising

♥♥♥♥♥♥♥♥♥

Rise up, sister. Rise to today's challenge. Come to Me and allow My power to change your fear to courage, your sorrow to joy, your anxiety to confidence. I never have—and never will—give you more of a challenge than you can successfully undertake.

Know this: I have given you the power to do all you are called to do. So swallow back that apprehension. Wipe away the sweat. Take a few deep breaths. Recite My name: "Jesus, Jesus, Jesus." And I will wing to your side. Be firm in the knowledge that there is nothing that, together, we cannot accomplish. I am not here to hinder—but to help. I hear your prayer. I understand your situation. I know the people involved. And I know what you can do when you have the confidence.

Let Me be your surety. I have never failed you before—and I will not fail you now. Let's move! Rise with the Son!

♥♥♥♥♥♥♥♥♥

"O Lord, I pray, please let Your ear be attentive to the prayer of Your servant, and to the prayer of Your servants who desire to fear Your name; and let Your servant prosper this day, I pray."

NEHEMIAH 1:11 NKJV

Soul Guard

♥♥♥♥♥♥♥♥♥

I am beside you—not to watch you stumble, but to catch you when you lose your balance. Not to see how far you can go without My help, but to strengthen you every step of the way. Consider Me your soul guard, King, and servant all rolled into one. Through Me, God sees you as the perfect creation. With Me, you cannot fail. Beside Me, you are undefeatable. Behind Me you are sheltered. Below Me, you are on solid ground.

I am the All-Powerful who strengthens you, the All-Present who never leaves you alone, the All-Knowing who answers every question you could ever imagine—and ones you have yet to think of. So do not worry about tripping over a stone. I can lift you above any impediments you may encounter. Together, we will win the race

of glory, victory, and love—here on earth and in heaven!

♥♥♥♥♥♥♥♥♥♥

Now to Him who is able to keep you from stumbling, and to present you faultless before the presence of His glory with exceeding joy, to God our Savior, who alone is wise, be glory and majesty, dominion and power, both now and forever. Amen.

JUDE 1:24–25 NKJV

Living Out the Truth

♥♥♥♥♥♥♥♥♥

It's one thing to read about Me, to learn to know Me. And it's another to actually follow in My footsteps. To live out the truth of My Word. But you must. The more you emulate Me, the more others will see Me in you, and the more light you will shine in this world. So cover yourself in the truth of My Word. Live in right standing with God. Soak yourself in My peace, and carry it with you into every situation. Continue to believe in Me, knowing the Word is alive and carries on its own mission. Understand the saving grace you have received, how I saved you before you even knew Me. All these things together make for one very powerful weapon—you and your life. The only time you may fail is when you attempt to live this life in your own power. So, woman, allow

Me into your heart. Abide in Me. And My power, My strength, My energy will keep you on the path to victory.

♥♥♥♥♥♥♥♥♥

Take all the help you can get, every weapon God has issued, so that when it's all over but the shouting you'll still be on your feet. Truth, righteousness, peace, faith, and salvation are more than words. Learn how to apply them. You'll need them throughout your life.

EPHESIANS 6:13–16 MSG

Power in Numbers

♥♥♥♥♥♥♥♥♥♥

You have been put in a family of God for a reason: there is power in numbers, for whenever and wherever two or three believers are together, I am there in the midst of them. And that is some astounding power that becomes even more potent and amazing when you gather to pray the Word, the scriptures. So when you are in the midst of a great battle, do not shrink back. Instead, move forward with another believer. Take the Word and give it life by speaking it aloud. Agree on the truth of the scripture. And pray, pray, pray. Pray for the salvation of unbelievers. Pray for the needs of your brothers and sisters in Christ. Pray for your family, the world, the persecuted, the maligned, the politicians, the rulers of nations, the imprisoned, the church, the ill of body, mind, and

spirit. Look at the world's woes and bring them to Me. When you do so, I and the Father will be moved into action. Meanwhile, Our hands are stilled as We await your word, your movement, your exercising of faith.

♥ ♥ ♥ ♥ ♥ ♥ ♥ ♥ ♥

God's Word is an indispensable weapon. In the same way, prayer is essential in this ongoing warfare. Pray hard and long. Pray for your brothers and sisters. Keep your eyes open. Keep each other's spirits up so that no one falls behind or drops out.

EPHESIANS 6:17–18 MSG

Limitless

♥♥♥♥♥♥♥♥♥

There is no limit to what we can do together when you put yourself in My hands, when you bow to the will of your Creator. Are you pliable? Do you believe the truth of My Word and the power of God behind it? Test Me in this, if you must. Take a promise from the all-knowing, all-powerful one. Claim it as your very own. Believe it as the Gospel truth. Live it in your life. Bend to its power and potency. Allow no doubts to creep in and tear it down, word by word, letter by letter. As was Mother Mary, become a true servant of the Lord. Give up your will to Mine and it will be according to what your Lord and Master has said. Move forward with no fear, knowing that the reality of My Word, the strength of God's truth, and the power of your willingness are an unbeatable combination, a limitless font of blessing.

♥ ♥ ♥ ♥ ♥ ♥ ♥ ♥ ♥

*With God nothing is ever impossible and
no word from God shall be without power
or impossible of fulfillment. Then Mary said,
Behold, I am the handmaiden of the Lord;
let it be done to me according to what you
have said. And the angel left her.*

LUKE 1:37–38 AMP

The Great Physician

♥♥♥♥♥♥♥♥♥♥

Are you troubled? Are you ill in mind, body,
spirit, or soul? If so, come unto Me. I will give
you rest—and more. I am the Great Physician
who has come to save you from every malady
known to woman. If you call upon Me for
healing, My power will automatically surge into
you. I will increase your energy with My own
Spirit. My Word will lift you up out of the pit.
My peace will soothe your frayed nerves. My
presence will comfort your anguished soul. I
have nothing but good news for you and your
own. So bring every request, every concern, every
obstacle, every problem, every person to Me.
And then leave them there! My arms can hold
them all! And there is nothing I cannot do to
aid you in each and every way. In My hands I

will change their sorrow to joy, their weakness to strength, their worry to serenity, their frustration to contentment. In My hands, in My hands, in My hands. Bring all. Leave all. And be at peace.

♥♥♥♥♥♥♥♥♥

And Jesus went about all the cities and villages, teaching in their synagogues and proclaiming the good news (the Gospel) of the kingdom and curing all kinds of disease and every weakness and infirmity.

MATTHEW 9:35 AMP

Perpetual Light

♥♥♥♥♥♥♥♥♥♥

My words light your path. Study them. Let them be a beacon as you sail the dark seas of life. Hone in on them so that you can find your way, the path you were meant to take. Memorize them. Doing so will help you to avoid the rocks that lie just beneath the surface of the waves. Live them so that you can stand up against the strong undertow that threatens to whisk you out into deeper, more treacherous waters. Allow My words to illume each and every channel you take.

Remember that the Word was made flesh and dwelt among you. I am your lifeguard. Keep your eyes on Me. Listen for My voice. Obey My every direction. Stay right in front of Me. I am your beacon. I am the One who lights your way, who dispels all gloom, who will never die. Yea, I

will continue to shine, shine, shine until I bring you home safe, until you reach the city of perpetual light that needs no moon or sun to shine on it, for God's glory gives it light and I, the Lamb of God, am its lamp.

♥♥♥♥♥♥♥♥♥

By your words I can see where I'm going;
they throw a beam of light on my dark path.
PSALM 119:105 MSG

Dream Provider

❤❤❤❤❤❤❤❤❤

Take each day's events as work you can do for Me. Never see anything as an interruption but as a potentially new assignment. Allow My power to flow through you so that you will have the strength and wisdom to meet all challenges. The only block in the channel may be yourself. Clear the way so that I can flow directly through you with no hindrance, such as fear, loathing, greed, pettiness, unforgiveness, malice, and the like. Do not be so focused on yourself and your own dreams, needs, and desires that you miss an opportunity to be the dream provider for someone else. This selflessness is the mark of a true woman of the Way. Work to joyfully move others ahead of yourself, and in so doing, you will find yourself even more blessed.

♥♥♥♥♥♥♥♥♥♥

*Do nothing from factional motives [through
contentiousness, strife, selfishness,
or for unworthy ends] or prompted by conceit
and empty arrogance. Instead, in the true spirit
of humility (lowliness of mind) let each regard
the others as better than and superior to himself
[thinking more highly of one another than you
do of yourselves]. Let each of you esteem and
look upon and be concerned for not [merely]
his own interests, but also each for the
interests of others.*

PHILIPPIANS 2:3–4 AMP

I Am

♥♥♥♥♥♥♥♥♥♥

I am the Son who brings you light each morning.
I am the cool glass of Living Water on a hot, dry
day. I am the beacon that guides you home from
foreign shores. I am the power you use when you
want to move mountains. I am the invisible wind
that makes the leaves dance in midair. I am the
love you see in a child's eyes. I am the words of
love whispered by the man of your dreams. I am
the riches you never imagined gaining at the end
of the rainbow. I am the deep sigh that refreshes
your weary bones. I am the peace that comes with
the embrace of a well-loved and loving friend. I
am the big brother who always has your welfare
first and foremost in his mind. I am the bloom of
beauty upon your favorite rose. I am the boat that
carries you from one destination to another. I am

the love that transcends all languages. I am the One you can trust above all others. You need not scramble to find Me, for I am always with you. I am the answer you have always sought. I am all things to you—and you are everything to Me.

♥♥♥♥♥♥♥♥♥

If you do not believe that I am He [Whom I claim to be—if you do not adhere to, trust in, and rely on Me], you will die in your sins. Then they said to Him, Who are You anyway? Jesus replied, [Why do I even speak to you!] I am exactly what I have been telling you from the first.

JOHN 8:24–25 AMP

Heavenly Ways

❤❤❤❤❤❤❤❤❤

There is no reason to be discouraged. You keep making the best decision based on your own knowledge at the time. But there is no way you can predict the future—much less people. So be gentle with yourself. Remember that My thoughts are not your thoughts. Nor are My ways necessarily your ways. And that's okay. That's how things are meant to be. Just continue to trust in Me. Know that everything will work out.

I have seen your beginning and will be a witness at your end. Take comfort in that thought. I will see you through it all. So set all worries aside. Stop berating yourself. Doing so will not help, that's for sure. In fact, it will only work to undermine the progress and assurance you have gained thus far. Just chalk it up to experience. And move

forward. I have a supreme plan for your life, and it is unfolding at this very moment. So leave all in My hands. I've already seen the opportunities that abound around the very next corner.

♥ ♥ ♥ ♥ ♥ ♥ ♥ ♥ ♥

"For My thoughts are not your thoughts,
nor are your ways My ways," says the LORD.
"For as the heavens are higher than the earth,
so are My ways higher than your ways, and
My thoughts than your thoughts."

ISAIAH 55:8–9 NKJV

Sleeping Blues Away

♥♥♥♥♥♥♥♥♥

Make every day a day of joy, for there can be no failure, no mistake, no second thoughts with Me in your life. Never fear. Never be discouraged. Trust Me until the last moment. I have promised that I will never forsake you.

But there is one thing you do need to do: acknowledge My presence in your life every day—and night. If you suffer from illness or pain, come give your body to Me. If you lose your job, house, or loved one, come and regain your confidence with Me. If you are not sure where to turn, come and get direction from Me. You see, I am always here. So it is your part to come to Me, to beckon Me. And I will help you to calm down and see straight. That's because I am the Lord of peace—a peace like none other you have ever experienced.

In all ways and in all days, I can restore your soul.
I can help you to rest. And I will watch over you
as you sleep your blues away.

♥ ♥ ♥ ♥ ♥ ♥ ♥ ♥ ♥ ♥

Now may the Lord of peace Himself grant you
His peace (the peace of His kingdom) at all
times and in all ways [under all circumstances
and conditions, whatever comes].
The Lord [be] with you all.
2 THESSALONIANS 3:16 AMP

373

Every Step of the Way

♥♥♥♥♥♥♥♥♥

A servant makes a living and a life by following the will of her master—and no other. So be sure to endeavor to seek My will. If you are at all confused, at the crossroads, don't know which way to turn, pray to our Father. Ask Him for wisdom as to My will and My way. Then pay close attention to all sides of the situation, all alternatives. Look for My hand. Listen for My voice. Know that I shall reveal all to you so that you will surely know which way to go. Ask boldly; then do not hesitate. Have no doubt that I will make the way clear. Once you are sure of your direction, be brave and move. You will find confirmation every step of the way.

♥♥♥♥♥♥♥♥♥♥

*If you don't know what you're doing, pray to
the Father. He loves to help. You'll get his help,
and won't be condescended to when you ask
for it. Ask boldly, believingly, without a second
thought. People who "worry their prayers" are
like wind-whipped waves. Don't think you're
going to get anything from the Master that way,
adrift at sea, keeping all your options open.*

JAMES 1:5–8 MSG

Self-Care

♥♥♥♥♥♥♥♥♥

Love yourself. Accept yourself exactly as you are, right now, in this moment. You are My creation. You are My sister. You are a wonder of wonders. Through you My light cannot help but shine. Stop beating yourself up. Instead, build yourself up.

Care for and be gentle with yourself. Fuel your gifts. Find a way to express yourself creatively, for you are an extension of the Master Creator. Find an outlet for your talents. Urge yourself to explore beauty, love, and kindness, within and without. At least once a day, find a way to nourish yourself—in mind, body, spirit, heart, and soul. For when you are strong within, you will have more power to strengthen those around you. You will have more love to share with one and all. In this way you will not only please God but be doing more to save yourself and others.

♥♥♥♥♥♥♥♥♥

*Do not neglect the gift which is in you,
[that special inward endowment] which was
directly imparted to you [by the Holy Spirit]. . . .
Look well to yourself [to your own personality]
and to [your] teaching; persevere in these things
[hold to them], for by so doing you will save
both yourself and those who hear you.*

1 TIMOTHY 4:14, 16 AMP

Surprise!

♥♥♥♥♥♥♥♥♥♥

Each day find a way to surprise yourself with Me. See Me in the devotion of a small child to its mother. See Me in the smile of a stranger on the street. See Me in the gratitude of a homeless person presented with food. See Me in the blue of the sky interspersed with random clouds holding the promise of rain. Feel Me in the Word of God that falls upon your ears and strikes a chord within. Feel Me in the love for a friend who has lost her job, home, husband, mother. Touch Me gently, as you would the petal on a flower. Feel Me in the water that rushes across your body in an early-morning shower. Experience Me as you cook a meal for your family, clean the bathroom, set a table. Find Me in the love for your husband, the excitement of a dream career, the anticipation

of blessings to give and receive. I am at work among you, loving you, blessing you, caring for you. Look for Me in anything. Recognize Me in everything. Surprise—I am everywhere!

❤ ❤ ❤ ❤ ❤ ❤ ❤ ❤ ❤ ❤

They all realized they were in a place of holy mystery, that God was at work among them. They were quietly worshipful—and then noisily grateful, calling out among themselves, "God is back, looking to the needs of his people!"
LUKE 7:16 MSG

Rejoice in Today!

♥♥♥♥♥♥♥♥♥

Today is a new day—made by God just for you! Receive it with joy—for that is how it has been given. No matter what the day brings, praise your God that you are here to live it! You have taken the good path the narrow way. But it is the joyous path all the same. For you have found God. And God is rejoicing in you!

I am the gate that leads to the marvelous pastureland of living in God's grace. Here with Me in this wonderful world you will be well fed, rested, watched over, and loved. So rejoice! Laugh! Love! There is no greater moment than this present one. There is no greater day than today. Do not fret about the future. Do not mourn the events of the past. Instead, find joy in the now. Find joy in your loved ones. Find joy in the job.

Today has been made by God and put into your hands. So make it a good day. Bless everyone you come into contact with—friend or foe! There is no greater way to spend the day than in love, love, love. And that is something worth celebrating!

♥♥♥♥♥♥♥♥♥♥

This is the day the LORD has made;
we will rejoice and be glad in it.
PSALM 118:24 NKJV

Saving Faith

♥♥♥♥♥♥♥♥♥♥

There is not one person who has never sinned—including yourself. So all are in need of forgiveness, from Me and you. For when a woman forgives, she begins healing the world one heart at a time. So begin today. Begin by forgiving yourself. Whether your sins have been great or small, it does not matter. There is enough forgiveness to go around. And the more forgiveness needed, the more love given. So allow your faith to save you. Simply forgive. Now. In this moment. Forget regrets. They are past history. Release yourself from the memory, the sorrow, the misgivings, the pain, the ache of yesterday, for what is done cannot be undone. But you must forgive and then move on, continuing to press forward. Let go of your unbelievably heavy burden. Leave it all at My feet. . . . Now breathe deeply. Know that I love you

very, very much. Know that it is your faith in Me that has saved you. Rest in that peace of mind.

Then, when you are ready, forgive all those you perceived as having wronged you, knowing that they, too, are only human and worthy of forgiveness. Let go of all animosity and bitterness. And you will find peace.

♥ ♥ ♥ ♥ ♥ ♥ ♥ ♥ ♥

"Therefore, I tell you, her many sins have been forgiven—as her great love has shown.
But whoever has been forgiven little loves little."
. . . Jesus said to the woman, "Your faith has saved you; go in peace."
LUKE 7:47, 50 NIV

383

Mental Meanderings

❤❤❤❤❤❤❤❤❤

Many people allow their minds to wander, never imagining what they may be saying to themselves throughout the day. But this cannot be. You must pay attention to the thoughts that are streaming through your mind. Are they uplifting? Are they disturbing? Are you putting yourself down with negative self-talk? Are you boosting your confidence with encouraging passages from My Word?

Woman, watch your words! Be vigilant in overseeing the messages in your mind. The thoughts of today will work to create your present—and your future! This should be no demeaning and meandering mental chatter. Do not allow your own thoughts to deceive you, to lead you into sin. Instead bring them

into the light. See what you are reflecting into this world! Change your thoughts and you will change your feelings, your reactions, and your world. You will find a new freedom in a new attitude, a new self growing more and more like Me every day! And that's a very good thing!

♥♥♥♥♥♥♥♥♥

You were taught, with regard to your former way of life, to put off your old self, which is being corrupted by its deceitful desires; to be made new in the attitude of your minds; and to put on the new self, created to be like God in true righteousness and holiness.

EPHESIANS 4:22–24 NIV

Victory!

♥♥♥♥♥♥♥♥♥

Get the concept clear in your mind that God is on your side! All His power is yours to exercise! So then, who can stand against Him? For God is the One who provided a natural-born son to an ancient, childless couple. God is the One who divided the Red Sea—and then reunited the waters. God is the One who sent angels to rescue Lot, Daniel, and My family! God is the One who allowed the earth to swallow major sinners, who sent manna from heaven to feed His people, and who through Moses brought water out of a rock. God is the One who empowered Me to heal people and work miracles, raised Me from the dead, allowed Me to walk through walls, and brought Me back to Himself.

You are more than just an ordinary woman.

You are a daughter of the King. You are a woman of the Way. God is more than on your side—He is a part of you, as am I. Remember that always—and victory will be yours!

♥♥♥♥♥♥♥♥♥

What then shall we say to [all] this? If God is for us, who [can be] against us? [Who can be our foe, if God is on our side?] . . . Yet amid all these things we are more than conquerors and gain a surpassing victory through Him Who loved us.

ROMANS 8:31, 37 AMP

387

Mountaintop Experiences

❤❤❤❤❤❤❤❤❤

Take some time each day, week, month, year to have a mountaintop experience. Get yourself away from the laundry, cooking, cleaning, office work, child rearing, and bankbook balancing, and spend time in a higher place. For on the mountain, you will find My dazzling light, inspiring you, strengthening you, leading you to a better self. This type of divine experience can be touched upon in your daily devotions, grasped at in your monthly Bible studies, and tasted in your Sunday communion. But to revel in it, to rest in it, to truly see the divineness of God, get yourself away, truly away in mind, body, spirit, and soul. Gather with other women of like mind. Have a time together with no "lights out." Instead, allow your soul to soar, your eyes to seek divine brightness, your heart